THE LEADER'S GUIDE TO

UNCONSCIOUS
BIAS

HOW TO REFRAME BIAS, CULTIVATE CONNECTION, AND CREATE HIGH-PERFORMING TEAMS

**PAMELA FULLER &
MARK MURPHY** WITH **ANNE CHOW**

Simon & Schuster
New York London Toronto Sydney New Delhi

Simon & Schuster
1230 Avenue of the Americas
New York, NY 10020

First Simon & Schuster hardcover edition October 2020

SIMON & SCHUSTER and colophon are registered
trademarks of Simon & Schuster, Inc.

For information about special discounts for bulk purchases,
please contact Simon & Schuster Special Sales at 1-866-506-1949
or business@simonandschuster.com.

The Simon & Schuster Speakers Bureau can bring authors to
your live event. For more information or to book an event,
contact the Simon & Schuster Speakers Bureau at 1-866-248-3049
or visit our website at www.simonspeakers.com.

Manufactured in the United States of America

10 9 8 7 6 5 4 3 2 1

Library of Congress Cataloging-in-Publication Data is available.

ISBN 978-1-9821-4431-9
ISBN 978-1-9821-4433-3 (ebook)

Contents

Preface

June 15, 2020

Between the time this manuscript went to the editors at Simon & Schuster on May 15, 2020, and when we received it back for review two weeks later, the world had changed. Or perhaps better said, the day-to-day struggles of the COVID-19 pandemic were overshadowed in the midst of global protests ignited by the tragic and unacceptable killings of Ahmaud Arbery, Breonna Taylor, and George Floyd. These most recent and senseless losses joined the long list of injustices toward Black people throughout history, resulting in a social tipping point. Affirming Black lives does not mean that this book is about racial injustice or public policy or even limited to bias as it relates to race. This book is our contribution to help advance a more inclusive world, where we can name and take responsibility for our own biases, use empathy and curiosity to more effectively connect with others, and choose courage to make positive changes at work. Discrimination, racial injustice, and injustice in any form—for example, based on race, color, sexual orientation, gender identity, national origin, disability, age, veteran status, family or marital status, physical appearance, education, and geography—have no place in the workplace or in society at large.

With that in mind, you may ask, *What is the connection between injustice and bias?* Bias is a natural part of the human condition and how our brains work. To be human is to have bias, and those biases—or preferences, as we'll describe in this book—do not have a value on their own. But they do impact our behavior, and that behavior can have benign, negative, or positive consequences. Uncovering and understanding our biases are the first steps to ensuring that our behavior does not limit our possibilities or the possibilities of those we work with.

Injustice is the ultimate limitation and does real harm to those directly and indirectly affected by it.

The need for a book such as this has long been present, but today addressing bias has transformed into one of the most important topics for individuals, communities, and organizations to confront—meaningfully, purposefully, and with a desire to listen, learn, engage, and do better. What follows is a framework for leaders at all levels in any role to enhance performance in themselves, their teams, and their organizations by understanding the nature of bias. In this book, we encourage each person to explore vulnerability, develop curiosity, and build empathy to move past negative biases and choose courage—all while applying best practices, strategies, and tactics to the Talent Lifecycle. We believe that these guideposts will help to build high-performing individuals, teams, and cultures in any organization and in any setting. We are proud of the content in these pages and invite you to engage with this work. Our intent is to ensure that everyone in the workplace can develop and take part in constructive dialogues about bias and inclusion while implementing actions that drive both progress and performance.

At a global FranklinCovey conference in 2011, Chairman and CEO Bob Whitman gave an inspiring speech sharing a list of simple tenets he had learned and followed over the course of his career. In that speech he said, "You must do the work your goals require." One of our goals is a more inclusive world, for ourselves, for our clients, and for the next generation of leaders. We are doing the work to achieve that goal and hope you will join us on the journey.

Pamela Fuller   Mark Murphy   Anne Chow

Foreword

At FranklinCovey, we recognize that leadership cannot be great if it isn't inclusive, if it leaves anyone behind. We believe that in order to achieve results, leaders must ensure that each member of their team can confidently state, "I am a valued member of a winning team doing meaningful work in an environment of trust." Without inclusion and the sincere intent to explore biases that could be unintentionally excluding some, and therefore limiting performance, this statement simply cannot be true.

As FranklinCovey's chief people officer, I am someone employees come to when they want an "unbiased" opinion or advice, and my responsibility is to support an inclusive and high-performing organization. And yet, I've learned that being truly unbiased is impossible, because we're human and have all been influenced by our past. What *is* possible is to recognize that we all have bias, carefully reflect on what ours might be, and determine if those biases are enhancing possibilities or getting in the way of performance. We can then choose how those biases impact our behavior and operate with as much objectivity and accuracy as possible. While this system is certainly far from perfect, it is what I try to do in all areas of my life.

A few years ago, our recruiting team was working with a senior manager who was in the process of hiring someone for a key position. After interviewing several candidates, he selected a woman who was already with our organization but in a different role. While market data had been used in determining the appropriate compensation for this position, this senior manager wanted to talk with me to rethink the compensation. When I asked him why, he said, "In looking at what she [the selected candidate] is currently making, this is going to be quite a jump for her." I asked him if he was having second thoughts about whether she met the qualifications or questioning the salary data provided, and he said no. "So help me understand your concern," I said.

He replied, "It just seems like such a big increase for her, and I never had a jump in pay like this."

This manager had a bias. After a long discussion, he realized his bias was about his own experience and a sense that no one should receive an increase in pay larger than one he'd ever received. Add to that all we know about the very real gender pay gap across corporate America, and his decision could have contributed to pay inequity at our firm. FranklinCovey conducts a pay equity audit each quarter to ensure this is not the case, but managerial decisions such as this can start to undo the positive results of those audits. This is just a single example out of many I've seen in my career where unconscious bias plays such a critical role in our judgment, decision making, possibilities, and performance.

At FranklinCovey, we have an intense and deliberate focus on diversity and inclusion, and have put a stake in the ground around the opportunities we have for improvement. We recognize the pivotal role our unconscious biases play in that effort. And while we continue to make significant progress, like many organizations, we recognize this is an ongoing, never-ending effort, and we still have a ways to go. Over the course of my career, I have seen that some leaders implicitly and passionately care about inclusion while others place less of a priority on this. They are well-intentioned but can't or don't see the connection between inclusion and results, or even their own personal responsibility to proactively build inclusion. There is simply no way to be a great leader if you don't confront your negative unconscious biases and make inclusion a hallmark of your leadership style. For a while, you may be able to hit your targets and draw on the force of your personality to get people to do what you want; you may even rise through the corporate ranks. But in the long run, true greatness requires a discerning, critical eye to be turned inward. Great leaders challenge themselves as much as they challenge others.

In *The Leader's Guide to Unconscious Bias*, authors Pamela Fuller, Mark Murphy, and Anne Chow have done an extraordinary job of defining what bias is, how it hurts or helps performance, and why it's so important for leaders, teams, and organizations. But they've also, with great wisdom and care, outlined exactly what to do about unconscious bias and how to course-correct when you see or feel it happening.

As I've read and reread their illuminating work, I've become more aware than ever of the unconscious biases I have that hinder my work and contributions. And I'm more focused on how to effectively influence those around me who are also slowed down by limiting biases.

As you read this insightful book, you too will find new and better ways of leading others, and will learn how to effectively address the challenges and opportunities bias presents in every area of your life.

Enjoy your read.

C. Todd Davis
Executive Vice President and
Chief People Officer, FranklinCovey

THE LEADER'S GUIDE TO

UNCONSCIOUS
BIAS

Introduction

To be human is to have bias. If you were to say, "I don't have bias," you'd be saying your brain isn't functioning properly!

Essentially, unconscious bias arises from the brain's capacity problem. We take in an astonishing eleven million pieces of information each second, but we can consciously process only about *forty* of those bits.*

To handle the gap, our brains build shortcuts to make sense of this information. We focus on the one angry customer instead of the hundreds of raving fans (negativity bias). We pay special attention to data that proves our strategy is working and gloss over data that casts doubt (confirmation bias). We unconsciously prefer the first job candidate we meet (primacy bias). And we simply like people who are like us (affinity bias).

These shortcuts can be a boon for time-strapped professionals, letting us make quick decisions without having to deliberate on every detail. They can also distort the facts, cause inaccurate judgments, and inhibit our professional performance and possibilities.

As logical and fair as we try to be, we are nearly always operating with a degree of bias, without ever being aware of it. But the sense that people who have biases are inherently ill-intentioned or morally flawed is one of the paradigms that stops us from making progress on this issue.

There's no shame in having unconscious bias; it's a natural part of the human condition that shows up in our decisions, our reactions, and our interactions with others. This is true in our relationships, our teams, and our organizations. We all have bias, so let's acknowledge it and begin to improve.

---

* Jin Fan, "An Information Theory Account of Cognitive Control." *Frontiers in Human Neuroscience* 8 (September 2, 2014): 680; https://doi.org/10.3389/fnhum.2014.00680.

I'll start.

I wear several hats at FranklinCovey, the global leader in helping organizations achieve results that require a change in human behavior. I consult with clients on broad leadership solutions, with an emphasis on diversity and inclusion; manage some of our most strategic accounts; and lead a team that supports those clients. As the lead architect of FranklinCovey's *Unconscious Bias* solutions, I help leaders build the skills to reframe bias, cultivate connection, and create high-performing teams. I'm also a first-generation American with roots in the Dominican Republic, Afro-Latina, the firstborn of eight children, and a wife.* I dabble in triathlons and 10Ks, and am always interested in a good story in print, on the screen, or over a glass of wine. I'm also the proud mama to two tiny humans, brown boys in America. We'll talk more about identifiers—mine and yours—as we move through this book. I spend a lot of time thinking about bias, both personally and professionally.

But none of that precludes me from having my own unconscious biases.

A few years ago, I won a large client contract, one of the biggest in the company at the time. We suddenly faced six months of work that needed to be completed in half that time to get a high-profile program off the ground. I was traveling every other week around the globe, balancing a two-year-old and a third grader at home, and working around the clock to ensure this project was a success. We needed more personnel, ASAP!

We began the hiring process for a new project manager, and after several rounds of interviews, we offered the job to Jordyn, a fantastic candidate with extensive customer-facing experience. She seemed ready for a new challenge and had an energy I related to. Jordyn accepted the job immediately—and then asked about the maternity leave policy. She was pregnant.

Did you groan when you read that? Admittedly, I groaned when I heard it!

I told her I would email information on benefits, ended the conversation, then immediately went to my leader, Preston, to vent my frustration. Why didn't this come up in the interview process? Should we have

---

* Please note that throughout this book, we've chosen to capitalize all racial and ethnic identities, including Afro-Latina, Black, White, and others.

offered the job to another candidate? Of course not—that would have been illegal, and Jordyn *was* the best candidate . . . but how on earth would she handle a new job and a new baby in the coming months? And maternity leave?! She hadn't even started yet, and I was already panicking about covering her absence.

Preston listened to my frustration and gently reminded me that we'd just had a pretty seamless maternity leave experience with another member of the team . . . me! Remember I mentioned I had a two-year-old at the time? My organization had given me flexibility in travel and work setting, and was patient with the occasional coo, babble, or cry on videoconference calls. (Frankly, they still are. Those sounds have given way to animal impressions, ninja battles, and couch jumping, and my boys still invade the home office from time to time!) In return, I'd created solid plans for coverage in my absence, ensured nothing fell through the cracks, and returned from leave with the energy to exceed expectations.

Preston told me, "There's no one better than you to navigate this successfully," then walked me through the process he'd used to prepare for my maternity leave. Having a plan resolved a lot of the tension I was feeling. I'd been lucky to have received empathy, confidence, and support from my leaders. And that was what I needed to offer this new employee; Jordyn deserved no less.

The mind-boggling thing about this experience was that I passionately believe workplaces achieve their highest performance when they allow their employees to be whole people, which includes taking the time to adjust to big life events like having a baby. I'm familiar with a wealth of research connecting parental leave and flexible workplace policies to better outcomes for parents, children, and results at work. I have a personal mission to develop diverse leaders and create inclusive workplaces that support them. I am *consciously* a champion of parenthood in the workplace!

But *unconsciously,* despite my own experience taking maternity leave and my values, I had a negative bias toward maternity leave, something I would not have recognized had I not been put in a circumstance for these feelings to come up. And when we're in situations that bring the unconscious to a heightened level of consciousness, we often find that our unconscious biases directly contradict our stated values.

As I write this, my team member's son just turned one. Did I miss her contribution while she was on leave? Absolutely! Did the many conversations we had leading up to her maternity leave give me some anxiety about how we'd fill the gap? Definitely! But I worked hard to ensure my negative bias didn't creep in, and we made a solid plan for her absence. While she was out, other members of the team had the opportunity to step up and perhaps perform outside of their comfort zone. As the old adage goes, "Absence makes the heart grow fonder." Boy, was I grateful when she returned!

As leaders, we've all likely encountered situations like this. I was recently on a call with an executive who had two employees taking overlapping paternity leaves, and he shared some of the same initial sentiments. But he ultimately supported both of them, and they returned from leave totally engaged. No leader is immune to the effects of bias. It is an ongoing reality—not something we learn once and conquer forevermore, but something we must continually examine and address.

Simply put, bias is a natural part of the human condition and can have a real impact on how we define our possibilities and those of others. The topic of unconscious bias can be a controversial one, fraught with opinions, politics, assumptions, and difficult interactions. But our experience and research have shown that bias is far more ubiquitous than we can even imagine, and it's impacting our organizational results—everything from culture, retention, recruitment, innovation, and profitability to shareholder return.

What Leaders Need to Know About Unconscious Bias

We define **bias** as a preference for or against a thing, person, or group compared with another. Biases may be held by an individual, a group, or an institution. We're sometimes conscious of these biases and can state them directly. Here's a common example: "We prefer to hire salespeople who are extroverted." Interestingly, data shows that the link between extroversion and sales success is essentially zero![*] Conscious biases are often beliefs we have simply decided are facts, regardless of the evidence.

---

[*] Murray R. Barrick, Michael K. Mount, and Timothy A. Judge. (2001). "Personality and Performance at the Beginning of the New Millennium: What Do We Know and Where Do We Go Next?" *International Journal of Selection and Assessment*, 9(1–2), 9–30.

Our focus in this book is **unconscious bias**, also called implicit or cognitive bias. Research shows that we have unconscious biases around gender, race, job function, personality, age/generation, socioeconomic status, sexual orientation, gender identity, family status, nationality, language ability, veteran status, culture, weight, height, physical ability, attractiveness, political affiliation, virtual/remote working, hair color—even the messiness of someone's desk or their posture.

These unconscious biases can have a positive, benign, or negative impact. A team leader might have a bias for collaborating: her default when assigned a new project is to reach outside of her team to seek feedback and test assumptions. She gets better results because of this bias, so it generally has a positive impact on her, her colleagues, and her organization. Other biases are quite benign, like a preference for working with or without music.

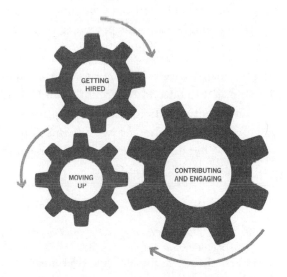

But many biases have a significant negative impact. As a result, these unconscious biases can limit professional opportunities for ourselves and others across the entire Talent Lifecycle. The Talent Lifecycle is the process of your career—all of the decision points that occur like getting hired, promoted, or selected for stretch opportunities. It also includes what kind of benefits you receive. We'll dive deeper into the Talent Lifecycle in Part 4 of this book.

Consider the following data:

- When five hundred hiring professionals were shown female candidates with a variety of body weights in a recent survey, only 18 percent said the heaviest-looking woman had leadership potential.[*] But is there a correlation between how much a woman weighs and her ability to lead? Of course not.

- Workers with strong regional accents are paid 20 percent less than those with a mainstream accent, according to research by the University of Chicago and the University of Munich. This bias against accents affects employees from the U.S. South, the working class in Britain, certain regions of Germany, and African Americans, to name just a few.[†]

- For people of color, the lighter your skin, the more likely you are to land a job, get promoted, be mentored, become CEO, and make more money. Lighter-skinned associates are more likely to be invited out to social events after work and befriended by their colleagues.[‡]

- Fifty-eight percent of CEOs in Fortune 500 companies are over 6 feet tall, compared to only 14.5 percent of all U.S. adult males.[§] Is there a correlation between height and the ability to run a company, or is it just perception? What do we unconsciously think power should look like? What does this mean for women and other people of generally smaller physical stature?

---

[*] FairyGodboss.com. (2017). *The Grim Reality of Being a Female Job Seeker*. PDF File. https://d207ibygpg2zlx.cloudfront.net/raw/uwpload/v1518462741/production /The_Grim_Reality_of_Being_A_Female_Job_Seeker.pdf.

[†] Jeffrey Grogger, Andreas Steinmayr, and Joachim Winter, *The Wage Penalty of Regional Accents*. NBER Working Paper No. 26719, issued in January 2020; https:// www.nber.org/papers/w26719.

[‡] Milagros Phillips, "Race: Inclusion and Colorism. How Understanding the History Can Help Us Transform." Forum on Workplace Inclusion Podcast, February 18, 2019; https://forumworkplaceinclusion.org/articles/p9/.

[§] Malcolm Gladwell, *Blink: The Power of Thinking Without Thinking*, Little, Brown, 2005.

None of us would post a job description consciously stating requirements for tall CEOs, slender high-potential leaders, posh accents, or
light-skinned people of color; yet, the data shows that these unconscious preferences are coming out in our behavior and impacting the
opportunities of others in a very real way. The bias I had against maternity leave—initially unconscious and brought to consciousness by my
hiring experience with Jordyn—would have negatively impacted how
I onboarded her, managed her, and engaged her in this new role. Her
performance undoubtedly would have suffered as a result.

This book will focus on unconscious biases that have negative impact on our opportunities and those of others in the workplace, and
we'll evaluate that impact through FranklinCovey's Performance Model.

You'll notice in the Performance Model that there are three separate
zones, each highlighting different experiences. Our goal, of course, is
to be in the High-Performance Zone, where people contribute at their
highest capabilities.

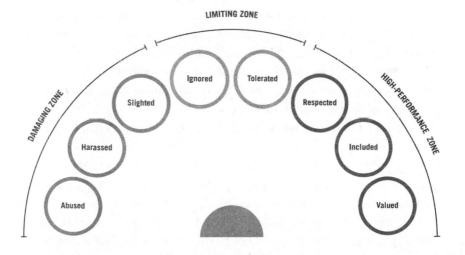

In the **High-Performance Zone,** people feel respected, included, and
valued, and are able to contribute their best. Historically, conversations
about diversity in the workplace focused on representation, or the composition of the workplace. Representation is important, but what you do
with that representation is also critical. Do those people feel included?

Do they feel like their perspectives are desired, that they have both a seat and a voice at the table?

In the **Limiting Zone,** people feel tolerated or ignored. Much of the work around diversity and inclusion has emphasized that we need to be tolerant of those who are different from us. But do any of us want to just be tolerated? It's not a great feeling. If my husband simply tolerated me, our marriage would be in pretty bad shape. Tolerance in the workplace is similarly less than optimal. Do you bring your best ideas forward when you're being tolerated or ignored? Do you want to?

In the workplace, people know when they're being ignored or tolerated—it's a very different feeling from being respected, included, and valued. As a woman of color operating in many predominantly White environments, I've felt the sting of that Limiting Zone. Often if I bring one of my male, White, or senior colleagues to a client meeting, the client will speak directly to my colleague, sometimes not even glancing my way, as if I'm not in the room at all and despite the expertise I might bring to that conversation. When something like this happened once, I dismissed it as probably not a big deal. But when it happened time and time again, I started to think, "Why am I being ignored? I've prepped for the meeting, connected in advance of the meeting to set expectations, and responded to the client's needs. Is there something else going on here?" Perhaps you've also experienced the Limiting Zone. What was the effect on your engagement and results?

Let's move into the **Damaging Zone.** Although we've discussed how bias is a normal part of how the brain works, we want to acknowledge that bias in the extreme can be incredibly damaging. In this zone, that level of bias can go even further to the point of illegality—harassment or abuse.

Much of diversity and inclusion (D&I) training in the workplace centers on the Damaging Zone, the most egregious of impacts. In my experience, people start to tune out when conversations about inclusion move to harassment and discrimination. Most of us don't consider ourselves capable of going that far. The consequence is that many of us couldn't imagine we'd be in the Limiting Zone either—and that's a mistake, because we all operate unconsciously sometimes. My experience in hiring a pregnant employee taught me that we can all slip into the Limiting Zone if we're not consistently exercising self-awareness. And once we're in the Limiting Zone, we can slip into the Damaging Zone if the organization or team dynamic normalizes that negative behavior. And we've seen that organizations across the board are dealing with a significant level of harassment and discrimination litigation—from well-intentioned but perhaps insensitive or ignorant managers finding themselves in career-ending litigation related to harassment and discrimination, to leaders who've clearly abused their power.

Every one of us has likely had experiences in each of the zones: times we felt respected, included, and valued; times we felt tolerated or ignored; and times we felt slighted, even harassed or abused. Our actions have also put *others* in each of these zones.

Having experience in each zone means we know what it feels like to be in each zone. And once we can identify what it feels like, we can recognize when it's happening and we can make positive progress on it.

Our Framework for Making Progress on Unconscious Bias

The good news is that our brains are wired not just for biases and preferences, but also for change and growth. It takes time and, more important, a conscious effort to create new neural pathways, ways of thinking, and habits. It's not easy, but it can happen.

To achieve this change, we have created a framework, the Bias Progress Model, that moves beyond awareness of unconscious bias to specific action, comprised of four parts: Identify Bias, Cultivate Connection, Choose Courage, and Apply Across the Talent Lifecycle.

Our goal with FranklinCovey's four-part Bias Progress Model is to not only define bias, but to provide a structure for making progress on

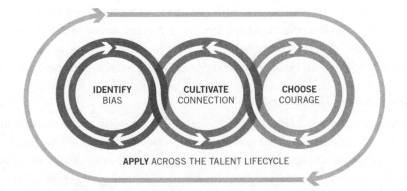

it. In this framework, each component fuels the others. The more you build each muscle, the more they work together to build your self-awareness, openness, potential for growth, and align to your purpose.

Identify Bias

To identify bias, we must first know what it is and the relationship between our biases and our identities, understand the basic neuroscience of why it happens, know some common terminology, and learn when we are most susceptible to bias traps. We must take on the intellectual pursuit of introspection and build self-awareness so we can look outside our own experiences to consider the experiences of those around us.

Cultivate Connection

Some of our deepest human needs are to belong, to feel connected, and to be understood. The second component of the Bias Progress Model is built around cultivating meaningful connection through empathy and curiosity. Empathy and curiosity are two sides of the same coin—the interpersonal and intellectual approaches to building connection. If we can meaningfully connect with others, we will often find ourselves surprised at what we learn, which is a clear check on biases and preconceived notions. Cultivating connection gives us a path through bias by getting to know people for who they truly are versus who we perceive them to be.

Choose Courage

We often think of courage as a brash and bold act. But courage is not always loud or ostentatious; it is sometimes quiet and careful. Through a combination of careful and bold courage, we can make progress on bias. This third part of the Bias Progress Model includes four ways to act with courage: the courage to identify bias, the courage to cope with bias, the courage to be an ally, and the courage to be an advocate.

Apply Across the Talent Lifecycle

As leaders, applying the Bias Progress Model in your relationships and to all your teams can fuel a shift to high performance. The ability to Identify Bias, Cultivate Connection, and Choose Courage as experienced through the Talent Lifecycle can transform the organization's performance for the better.

When we hear about the war on talent, retaining top talent, and ensuring collaboration and innovation, the lever through which an organization can achieve those things is the Talent Lifecycle. We often think of the Talent Lifecycle as a realm of law and HR policy; but ensuring a strong Talent Lifecycle requires *all* leaders to go beyond the regulations, policies, and procedures found in the company's handbook. This final component of the Bias Progress Model, the surrounding piece of the model, ensures that the policies live off the page and support real organizational results.

We'll continue to unpack and explore the Bias Progress Model throughout this book. The book is organized into four parts:

Part 1: Identify Bias
Part 2: Cultivate Connection
Part 3: Choose Courage
Part 4: Apply Across the Talent Lifecycle

The Bias Progress Model is drawn from FranklinCovey's *Unconscious Bias: Understanding Bias to Unleash Potential* work session, which has been field-tested by thousands of leaders at all levels in many industries, including healthcare, banking, technology, oil and gas, law enforcement, government, and retail. As the lead architect of this work session, I've had the privilege of constructing and delivering this program to numerous participants, and have worked with a brilliant team of global consultants to refine this material based on their feedback implementing the content. I've found that across industries and locations, leaders and organizations encounter bias that inhibits performance, but they're unsure what to do about it. This *Leader's Guide* is written to solve that problem.

What is a book about bias and inclusion without diverse perspectives? I'm also joined by my two coauthors, Mark Murphy and Anne Chow. While my voice guides the main text for ease of reading, we are truly a team of collaborators. You will also see insights and experiences in Mark's and Anne's voices inset throughout the pages. Mark

Murphy, a twenty-eight-year senior consultant at FranklinCovey, certifies FranklinCovey's consultants and clients to deliver this content around the globe. You'll hear his stories and perspective from working with clients across multiple industries. Because of his own life experiences and extensive global travel, Mark is passionate about inclusion and bias and helps clients build inclusive cultures. As a member of the LGBTQ+ community, Mark has experienced firsthand the impact these principles have on people's abilities to bring their whole self to work.

Anne Chow, CEO of AT&T Business, a more than $30 billion division of AT&T that on its own would qualify as a Fortune 50 company, lends her experience in leading global teams and business transformation over the course of more than three decades in the telecom and tech industries. Anne started with AT&T as an engineer and has since held more than a dozen roles across the company, culminating with her appointment as the first female CEO of AT&T Business and the first woman of color CEO in AT&T's over 140-year-old history. She brings her vast insights concerning leading at all levels, managing organizational change, serving clients, and driving cultural change. Anne is a proud second-generation Asian American, whose parents emigrated from Taiwan to pursue the American dream, and she's passionate about the power of authenticity and communication to build inclusive, high-performing organizations. She's also a Juilliard-trained pianist and brings a sense of excellence and purpose to all she does, including her contributions to this book.

What to Expect

It is our hope that at the end of this book, you will feel empowered to deploy vulnerability, empathy, curiosity, and courage to make progress in the face of bias and build a diverse, equitable, and inclusive organization. If you're a diversity, equity, and inclusion professional whose role is dedicated to this pursuit, we hope this book reinvigorates your efforts, gives you additional language to build allies and stakeholders, and inspires clear actions to make progress. If you are skeptical of diversity and inclusion as a critical leadership competency, we hope this book will open your mind to these ideas, if even just a bit. And for everyone in between, we've worked to build an accessible tool kit that expands your leadership to always consider inclusion. Here are two best practices to get the most out of our book:

- **Do the work.** You'll find an exercise or tool at the end of each chapter, segmented into reflections for individuals and application for leaders. We encourage you to grab a pen and write your answers in the book. This takes a bit of time and effort, but completing the tools is the difference between simply learning about this content and implementing it to achieve better results.

- **Explore further.** You may read about ideas that don't feel intuitive to you. Pursue those questions through further exploration. That might mean engaging with someone in your network with a different perspective or background, or seeking out perspectives available in other forms of media—books, podcasts, or websites.

So with that context in mind, let's tackle some of the burning questions you might have about this material.

With all that leaders are responsible for, is making progress on unconscious bias really that important?

There's a wealth of data that demonstrates the connection between bias and performance. Reducing bias can help your team and organization achieve better results—period.

Bias can inhibit decision making, performance, innovation, and results in the workplace. And a big part of our mandate throughout this book is to think about how bias can either inhibit or accelerate performance. Employees who perceive themselves to be the target of bias are three times as likely to withhold ideas, be disengaged, and leave within a year.[*] If you've been on the receiving end of bias, this makes perfect sense. If you haven't, it can be shocking to consider that you might have unknowingly contributed to those perceptions or outcomes.

There is no idea more fundamental to performance than how we see

---

[*] *Disrupt Bias, Drive Value.* Center for Talent Innovation, 2017; https://www.talent innovation.org/_private/assets/DisruptBias-DriveValue_Infographic-CTI.pdf.

and treat each other as human beings. This is why understanding and often challenging bias matters.

Is this topic just a trend?

The demographics are clear. We are living in a global world that requires us to collaborate and partner across many facets of identity.

Addressing unconscious bias is as much of a trend as innovation, change, and leadership skills—wait, exactly, they're not! They aren't always as visibly profitable on a balance sheet as revenue and cost, but these strategic competencies make all the difference in an organization's ability to achieve results. As long as there are organizations to run, we will need to contend with bias and its effect on performance.

Is a lot of this more about politics or being politically correct?

As bias becomes a deeper part of societal consciousness, we might feel like we're being put under a microscope. We all have strong feelings about our own perspectives, which sometimes come forward as politics. I believe that for some people, exploration of diversity, inclusion, and bias does align to their politics. But I do not believe these topics are political ones. In this book, our approach to bias is laser-focused on the connection between bias and workplace performance.

Our goals for this book do not include tokenism, political correctness, or limits on the opportunities of anyone. You will not walk away from this book with a list of what you can and cannot say, nor is it our intent to police anyone's language or thoughts. The goal of exploring and reframing bias is not to censor you but to build your ability to understand and be understood as you connect with others.

Doesn't this create reverse bias?

We would argue that there is no such thing as reverse bias. Bias is a preference for or against a thing, person, or group compared with another. Whether that bias is positive or negative, or about one group or another, it is bias.

Throughout this book, you will see examples that cross a robust spectrum of identities and circumstances. Will you read examples focused on race and gender? Absolutely. Will you also read examples focused on personality, job function, appearance, remote workers, accents, and education? Yes, plus many more.

Ultimately, we have all had an experience with bias, a way in which bias has impacted us negatively or positively. Bias impacts you if you have an unpopular opinion; if you're left-handed, attractive, or disorganized; if you are an introvert or a risk-taker. It impacts you if you're a veteran or a resident of a rural community or if you have a disability. And it impacts you based on your race, gender, sexual orientation, gender identity, and IQ.

Exploration of bias is not about villainizing one group over another or making anyone feel guilt, shame, or fear. It's about making progress on our biases and understanding how they limit possibilities for us or others. Our hope is that this content creates awareness, connection, and commitment.

Rudine Sims Bishop, the Ohio State Professor Emerita of Education who is commonly known as the mother of multicultural children's literature, wrote: "Books are sometimes windows, offering views of worlds that may be real or imagined, familiar or strange. These windows are also sliding glass doors, and readers have only to walk through in imagination to become part of whatever world has been created or recreated by the author. When lighting conditions are just right, however, a window can also be a mirror. Literature transforms human experience and reflects it back to us, and in that reflection we can see our own lives and experiences as part of the larger human experience. Reading, then, becomes a means of self-affirmation, and readers often seek their mirrors in books."[*] We hope you find some windows, sliding doors, and mirrors in this work. Embracing those possibilities will enhance your experience throughout this book and the application of these insights in every aspect of your life.

---

[*] Rudine S. Bishop, "Mirrors, Windows, and Sliding Glass Doors," in *Collected Perspectives: Choosing and Using Books for the Classroom,* ed. Hughes Moir, Melissa Cain, and Leslie Prosak-Beres. Boston: Christopher-Gordon Publishers, 1990.

Everybody's biased. The truth is, we all harbor unconscious assumptions that can get in the way of our good intentions and keep us from building authentic relationships with people different from ourselves. By becoming more self-aware, we can control knee-jerk reactions, conquer fears of the unknown, and prevail over closed-mindedness. In the end, our central message is that you are not the problem—but you can be the solution.

—Dr. Tiffany Jana, author, CEO, and social entrepreneur

Part 1: Identify Bias

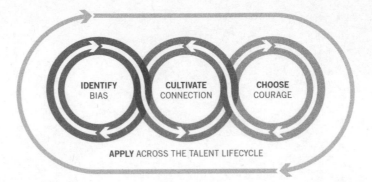

The data around bias can be daunting—they're macro numbers that feel beyond our control. But we must remember that those big numbers are the accumulation of many individual actions, and we can affect those.

While I can't personally plant a billion trees to combat carbon emissions, I can recycle and ride my bike more often. Likewise, we can implement small behaviors to impact bias, specifically as it relates to enhancing our own possibilities and those of our team members, colleagues, and clients. The cumulative impact of all our changed behavior can make a huge difference.

A colleague of mine who works in film once told me that if a camera operator shifts the lens by just 5 degrees, it completely reframes the shot. Likewise, our exploration of bias is not focused on the monumental shifts. Instead, we will focus on the power of meaningful and possible small changes to fundamentally impact our results. Each part of our Bias Progress Model will begin with a frame/reframe statement to shift our mindset by a metaphorical 5 degrees.

Frame/Reframe

Frame:	Reframe:
I am not biased. I view things objectively.	Bias exists in everyone, including me. I actively think about how bias is at play in the choices I make.

The frame assumes we are each infallible. Even the smartest, most capable, most decisive of us have bias. It's part of our internal programming. The reframe just acknowledges that reality and allows us to expand our behavior, reactions, and decisions to account for our biases and enhance our performance.

The Principle of Self-Awareness

Each component of our four-part framework is also associated with a principle. The principle of Identify Bias is self-awareness, that uniquely human capacity for introspection. The word "self-awareness" may be overused, but it involves more than just deciding you're an introvert or an extrovert or taking a general personality assessment.

For the purposes of this book, we define "self-awareness" as the intellectual pursuit of introspection. Increased self-awareness can enable us to identify our biases. Building this muscle of self-awareness, in this context, means that we can pause between receiving information and responding to it emotionally. We can take a step away from those feelings to understand *why* we're feeling that way and examine if the feelings are productive.

One of the reasons our minds work against self-awareness is because it's hard to admit that we have areas where we could improve. But when we practice self-awareness, we are constantly becoming more knowledgeable about ourselves. When we build self-awareness, we stop acting automatically and start making better decisions.

So how do we shift from the frame to the reframe and tap into our ability to become self-aware in order to identify bias? The four chapters of Part 1 are a guide to doing just that. We begin by exploring our own identity. Then we attempt to understand the neuroscience involved. The next step is to recognize when we are in one of the three bias traps. Finally, we embrace mindfulness as a strategy for continuously honing that principle of self-awareness.

Chapter 1: Explore Identity

Identities come, first, with labels about why and to whom they should be applied. Second, your identity shapes your thoughts about how you should behave; and third, it affects the way other people treat you. Finally, all these dimensions of identity are contestable, always up for dispute: who's in, what they're like, how they should behave and be treated.*

—Kwame Anthony Appiah, professor of philosophy and law, New York University

The first step in identifying bias is to know ourselves and examine how personal identity influences and is influenced by bias.

Our identities are comprised of everything that's been poured into us over our lifetimes. These shaping influences come from everywhere, a multitude of sources our brains aggregate to develop a particular sense of self for each of us, and in some ways, a decision matrix for how we interact with the rest of the world.

In FranklinCovey's Identity Model, the sources that comprise our identities include:

- **Information.** What we listen to, what we read, what we hear, what we watch—all of that information shapes our world views, perspectives, and biases. With the use of artificial intelligence and algorithms in social media—plus our brains' inherent confirmation bias—we're

---

* Kwame Anthony Appiah, *The Lies That Bind: Rethinking Identity*. New York: Liveright Publishing, 2018.

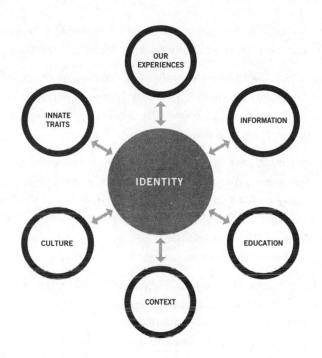

getting more and more information thrown at us that affirms our existing beliefs, rather than taking in a wide swath of information.

- **Education.** An attorney thinks about things differently than someone who went to school for criminal justice does. A scientist looks at everything through the lens of the scientific method; an MBA is trained to solve strategic problems. Our level of education (be it a high school diploma, a trade degree, a bachelor's degree up through a doctorate or other certification), our field of study and the specific educational institutions we attended contribute to our sense of self—and our preferences and biases.

- **Context.** Identity can change as our situation changes: where we live, our religious practice, our situational contexts at work—for example, moving to a new organization or team. My identity today as a professional and a parent is certainly different from my view of myself when I was a college sophomore. Veterans and others who serve in uniform often experience this sharp change in context. The uniform can form a core part of their identities, an indication of the service they're performing for their nation and their role as warriors. Moving into civilian contexts can challenge that identity, for example.

- **Culture.** This could be race, religion, ethnicity, or geography. Those cultural elements can have significant bearing, whether you're from a state with a big, bold personality like Texas or from a relatively small ethnic group like the Hmong Americans.

- **Innate Traits.** Some of us are risk-takers; some of us are cautious. Some of us are nurturers; some of us aren't. As an introvert, I usually order room service and go to bed after a long day of interacting and consulting with clients, and that, as a result, impacts my experiences of travel for work. We have innate preferences that also can contribute to bias and to the way we see circumstances and situations.

- **Our Experiences.** How many stories have you started with "Remember the time when . . ."? Our experiences stay with us, leaving a lasting impression. The experience of relocating across the country or traveling to a new one, of completing an ultramarathon, or of working for an incredibly inspirational leader—these varied experiences influence how we see future experiences and the choices we make.

These are components of your identity. And you'll notice that in FranklinCovey's Identity Model, these arrows go two ways. These elements influence our identity, *and* our identity influences them back, both creating biases.

Information is a perfect example of this dynamic. My parents grew up under a fascist dictator in the Dominican Republic. My father looked at Cuba as a model, because they overthrew their fascist dictator, Fulgencio Batista, in the 1950s. Since then, his politics have influenced my own. That part of my identity fuels the information and media I seek. In turn, that media consumption reinforces, confirms, and influences my identity, and shapes my preferences and biases. Of course, recognizing this narrow lens means I need to proactively broaden it by seeking out media across the political spectrum and making sure my network includes people who disagree with me politically. Admittedly, this is easier said than done, but it's also self-awareness—recognizing my identity-based bias and proactively counterbalancing it.

The Identity Model is a two-way street, and it is dynamic, constantly being influenced by new components of the model. The sort of information I consumed when I worked in the nonprofit sector early in my career was focused on fundraising and grant strategies. Today most of what I consume professionally is focused on learning and development, diversity, and inclusion. My preferences and biases have shifted accordingly.

The Whole-Person Paradigm

When we hear the word "Haiti," we often think of a common context: widespread poverty, exacerbated by the catastrophic earthquake in 2010. But Chimamanda Ngozi Adichie, author and winner of a MacArthur Genius Grant, points out in her TED talk that there's danger in telling a single story. We nearly always define Haiti as the poorest country in the Western Hemisphere; we rarely define it as the first Black independent nation in the Western Hemisphere.* And that story, that limiting narrative, is damaging over time.

When we consider identity, we might feel more vulnerable about some components than others, prouder of some than others. Sometimes those components are clear at first glance, but sometimes they are not.

ANNE

None of us are one-dimensional. You would no doubt look at me and think, "She's a woman and she's Asian." You might notice my stature or my clothes. If you worked with me, you would probably also say, "She's passionate about customers, she's a business leader, and she deeply cares about her people and her relationships."

I am also a mom, a wife, a former pianist, a proud Gen Xer, and I live at the intersection of all the unique experiences I've had throughout my

---

* Chimamanda Ngozi Adichie, "The Danger of a Single Story." TED talks, July 2009; https://www.ted.com/talks/chimamanda_adichie_the_danger_of_a_single _story.

life. This multifaceted nature of my identity applies to all of us. Some of these components of my identity have associated stereotypes. It's important not to fall into those stereotypes about myself and to consider what stereotypes I have about others. They are limiting and can often be harmful, and most certainly, they distract us from truly valuing the diverse skills, experiences, and potential of others.

Have you ever heard these assertions?

- Girls aren't good at math.
- Men are so insensitive.
- Most Asians/Blacks don't communicate well.
- He/She/They aren't as sharp as they used to be when they were younger.
- Short people can't play volleyball/basketball/command a stage.

Underlying each of these comments is a stereotype. And for sure, they are hurtful to the individuals and communities they reference. In a work environment, they are also harmful to the performance of both individuals and teams, as they can presuppose a dynamic that is suboptimal, hence negatively impacting the most fulsome contribution and performance. One of my favorite quotes on this topic is from Martina Navratilova, considered one of the best female tennis players of all time. She once said, "Labels are for filing. Labels are for clothing. Labels are not for people."

We are all so much more than a single story, but in day-to-day interaction, we can be limited to a single component of our identity, one that ignores the complexity we each bring to the table as whole people. Someone can at the same time be an attentive parent and a high-performing employee traveling the globe. Someone can be a soft-spoken person and a visionary and impactful leader. Someone can appear perfectly composed and be struggling with a significant emotional disability such as anxiety or depression.

A common image used to describe this complexity is the iceberg. On average, about 10 percent of an iceberg is above the surface; 90 percent is below the surface, invisible to us. Identity is similar. When two people meet or when we encounter a group of people together, we can see only a small part of their identities—often age, race, gender, culture, physical appearance, and potentially physical ability or religious affiliation, among others.

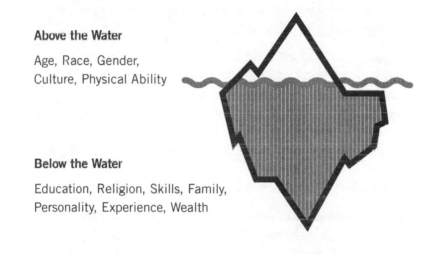

Above the Water

Age, Race, Gender,
Culture, Physical Ability

Below the Water

Education, Religion, Skills, Family,
Personality, Experience, Wealth

Much of what we can't see is incredibly substantive and formative of our identity: education, some religions, skills, family status, less visible facets of personality, experience, wealth. As we recall the statistics in the Introduction, many of the limiting biases come from the 10 percent of visible identity—age, race, gender, culture, physical ability. There is often a disconnect between what people perceive about us and how *we* define ourselves. Have you experienced this?

Each of us is a whole person with complex identities, engaging with other whole people with similarly layered identities. The danger of a single story is not just the ways we limit our own possibilities, but also how we might apply that single lens to others.

To identify bias, we must dig deeper into identifiers both above and below the waterline and do the heavy work of introspection. Then we can understand how those identifiers affect our experience with bias.

MARK

I spend a lot of my time facilitating our *Unconscious Bias* work sessions with clients. As often is the case, I was working with a client, and the human resources director was in attendance. She shared that being in HR can be very isolating in an organization. When she walks into a room, people often change their conversation, lower their volume, or even stop talking altogether. She's often identified with her role first, even to the exclusion of her name—people will say, "Here comes HR," or "Be careful—HR's in the room!"

Have you caught yourself doing something similar? It can seem quite natural to default to stereotypes about job functions. Several years ago, I was asked to speak to a group of a hundred accountants in Oklahoma. Sounds exciting, right? If you answered no, you likely have some of the biases I had walking into that room. For me, several biases kicked in about accountants (and Oklahoma). In all honesty, I was dreading the day. I was expecting to have to pull teeth with a deadpan group, and to leave exhausted and disheartened by my efforts.

I couldn't have been more wrong. An energetic group, they were highly engaged and eager to participate, and the day flew by. Since then, I've become much more deliberate about checking the assumptions I bring into a work session.

Finding the Origin Stories of Our Biases

A primary goal of exploring bias is to bring the unconscious to consciousness so that we can improve the quality of our decisions and relationships. Once we bring the unconscious forward and can name it, we can also do some analysis of it. Does this bias serve me? Does it limit my possibilities or the potential of those around me? Does it impact an upcoming decision I need to make? And if it does have impact, how do I avoid making decisions or behaving negatively in response to that bias in the future? If we can articulate the origin story of that bias—where it comes from in our life—we are more likely to consider that story next time we encounter that bias.

For example, a bias that I speak about quite often is around education. For a long time, I looked at education first as I reviewed résumés, and I valued prestigious degrees from prestigious institutions. My husband pushed my perceptions here. He greatly valued individuals who took a less traditional route to a four-year degree: working, junior college, part-time college, transfer students. His argument was that the tenacity and determination it takes to complete a four-year degree while also working was a much better indicator of work ethic than prestige. This had me thinking about where my education bias came from. As the child of immigrants from the Dominican Republic, education, particularly a degree from a prestigious institution, was a value ingrained in me my whole life. I was raised to believe that getting the best education possible demonstrated my work ethic. So my husband and I both value a strong work ethic, but my origin story had me looking for it in résumés in a limited fashion. In recognizing this, I can now review résumés for evidence of a strong work ethic in its many forms: accomplishments, promotions, research—any number of ways beyond where someone went to school and how many degrees they have.

ANNE

What do you picture when you think of a salesperson?

Before I became one, I'll admit the image that popped up in my mind was of a stereotypical used-car salesman. When I thought of my professional life, sales was the furthest thing from my mind. More than five years into my career, I found myself in a sales role, and surprisingly, I fell in love with it. I had not anticipated the power and clarity of waking up every day with a clear mission to serve my clients and grow relationships in both a figurative and a literal way.

Do you have biases about different professions—salespeople, lawyers, accountants, teachers, engineers, software developers, even interns? Beneath all of those titles are complex and unique human beings. Functional bias means we ignore that fact and revert to a stereotype about the position. When people start referring to "us" and "them"—for example, sales versus marketing or acquisitions versus operations—that's a sure sign that functional bias is getting in the way.

As a leader, consider your language. Are your words inclusionary beyond the boundaries of your team? Do you frame and reframe a perspective, putting yourself in someone else's position? When you hear "they" language, especially in the context of barriers, issues, conflicts, and concerns, do you encourage your team to think about who "they" are and why "they" might be reacting or acting in such a way? Even seemingly minor comments such as "We all wear the same badge" or "We all want the same outcome" can help encourage those around you to work through functional bias in a constructive way.

Pay special attention to the origin stories of your self-limiting biases. A few years ago, I had a mentoring dinner with an executive. As we connected, I spent about ten minutes describing myself—or at least how I saw myself at the time. I leaned into my work ethic and strategic mind, but I described myself in a way that would have you believe I was incapable of forming good working relationships. "I'm a lot," I said. "I'm rather intense, and I know people don't like that."

This leader's jaw dropped. She said without hesitation that she didn't know what I was talking about. She went on to say she thought I was delightful, and I had a reputation across the company of being personable and capable. We had a long conversation about why I'd labeled myself as unlikable.

As I considered how much energy I'd given to this false idea, I was horrified. This thought was born of a self-limiting bias that I wasn't likable, which came from prior work environments where I'd worked hard and accomplished a lot, but never felt like I belonged or that I was part of the "cool clique." Now when I think about interactions with new colleagues, clients, or stakeholders and this belief starts to creep in, I remember the origin story of that self-limiting bias. Then I remind myself I no longer work in those places and I shouldn't behave as if I do. I'll only limit myself.

MARK

I spent the first half of my life believing I wasn't enough, that I probably would never be enough, and that at my core, I was unworthy of success or even happiness. Talk about self-limiting bias. I grew up in an environment that had some pretty set ideas of what constituted worthiness—and being gay certainly didn't fit that ideal. It was a part of my identity that wasn't clear from my physical appearance. It was certainly below the waterline as we consider the iceberg model, and I worked hard to keep it that way.

After many years of internal struggle and therapy, I've now fully embraced this important component of my identity. But there are still aspects of that origin story of inadequacy that continue to have a limiting effect on me. I overcompensated by leaning into perfectionist tendencies. If everything could just appear perfect, no one would know my secret. In fact, they'd see me as worthy, even though I didn't feel that way inside.

It took a dear friend and colleague to courageously help me understand how limiting this origin story about my worthiness, or lack thereof, had been. She said with complete kindness: "Mark, your desire to be perceived as perfect keeps you from learning and growing. You're afraid to try anything new because you won't look perfect doing it. Learning and growing is a messy process, so you have to be willing to stumble around some to ultimately succeed." That was an epiphany for me.

It's a struggle I continue with even today. Our self-limiting biases are very powerful and can be incredibly damaging when left unchecked. And sometimes it takes someone who cares enough about us to help us rewrite that story.

Chapter 1: Explore Identity
Reflection for Individuals

Discover "I am" Statements

1. Dig into your own identity. Complete ten "I am" statements about who you are representing both "above the water" (age, race, gender, culture, physical abilities) and "below the water" identifiers (education, religion/spirituality, skills, family relationships, personality, defining experiences, etc.). Don't overthink these; just jot down the first things to cross your mind.

I am...

I am...

I am...

I am...

I am...

I am...

I am...

I am...

I am...

I am...

2. Think carefully about those identifiers that may fuel an unconscious (or conscious) bias toward others. Put an X next to those identifiers. For example, an avid reader may hold a negative bias toward those who never pick up a book or even listen to an audiobook. Be honest about how your identifiers influence how you make decisions, view relationships, or see others.

3. Put an O next to the identifiers that you feel could or have made others biased toward you. There might be identifiers where you have both an X and an O.

Write an Origin Story

4. Consider the correlation between your identity and potential or uncovered biases. Do they limit possibilities or expand them? Are they serving you well, or getting in the way of what you're trying to achieve? Do they influence you to put off decisions, or lure you to rush into actions you often regret?

....

....

....

....

5. Analyze how your "I am" statements connect to what you value and how they ultimately make you feel (vulnerable, proud, indifferent, etc.).

....

....

....

....

6. Pick an "I am" statement with an X and list where it may have come from (media, parents, peers, society, education, context, culture, innate trait, etc.).

....

....

....

....

7. Identify any facets of your identity (personality, experiences, etc.) that may have reinforced your uncovered or potential bias.

....

....

....

....

Remember that all the components of our identifiers make us biased in some way toward others. We lay our values over other people, and that potentially makes us susceptible to bias, just as other people are laying their values over us.

Chapter 1: Explore Identity
Application for Leaders

Our biases impact how we as individuals relate and engage with other people and circumstances, how we make decisions and ascribe value. When we serve in a leadership role, the immediate recipients of our biases are our teams.

1. Choose the origin story you wrote on the previous pages and overlay it on your team. Perhaps it's an origin story about priorities, integrity, ambition, work ethic, the role of family in our lives, or something else.

2. Write the names of your direct reports below. (If you don't have any, consider your team of peers instead.)

....

....

....

3. For each name above, consider how your origin story impacts how you see this person, what kind of relationship you have with them, and how you make decisions with or regarding them. If it produces a negative outcome, how does recognizing your bias allow you to change your thinking and behavior? (Write your answers below.)

....

....

....

....

....

4. To make the most of this process, repeat this exercise with customers, stakeholders, and colleagues.

Chapter 2: Understand the Neuroscience

If you're aware of [unconscious bias], then you can bring to bear all of your critical skills and intelligence. . . . We all have the ability to control it.

—Dr. Lasana Harris, senior lecturer in experimental psychology, University College London

Remember those middle school word problems about how fast a train is going? American researchers gave a group of individuals a similar set of word problems.* They gave them a baseline test on their math skills, then a problem to solve about skin care and a problem to solve about gun control. The results were fascinating. If the answer to the gun-control problem contradicted the individual's political beliefs, the participants couldn't solve it. This was true of both conservatives and liberals. Their ability to solve the problem changed based on the beliefs they held. Their literal ability to do math, their thinking brain, changed based on the context of the problem.

And remember that baseline math test? The researchers found that the better the participants were at math, the more difficult it was for them to solve a problem that contradicted their political beliefs. Surprising, right?

Like many of you, I consider myself a pretty sharp person. So it was

---

* Dan M. Kahan, Ellen Peters, Erica Dawson, and Paul Slovic, "Motivated Numeracy and Enlightened Self-Government." *Behavioural Public Policy* 1 (September 8, 2013): 54–86; Yale Law School, Public Law Working Paper No. 307; https://ssrn .com/abstract=2319992 or http://dx.doi.org/10.2139/ssrn.2319992.

mind-blowing to me that my smarts and capability would actually make me *less* likely to accept facts I didn't want to be true. But as I considered this possibility, it made sense. Think of it as habit. If we're in the habit of being right, the systems in our brains will support and confirm that.

Some of our beliefs can limit our own possibilities and abilities, and others can limit how we see and define the possibilities and abilities of others—the false belief that salespeople must be extroverts, for example. These beliefs can be so deeply ingrained in our brains that we literally can't believe they are wrong, even when faced with facts. Making progress on bias often requires us to examine the repercussions of our most deeply held thoughts and beliefs.

How Our Brains Create Bias

Remember that bias is how the brain gets us through each day without being paralyzed by the onslaught of information coming at us. What is actually happening in our brains that leads to bias? To answer that question, we need to understand the three major systems in the brain: primitive, emotional, and thinking.

The **primitive brain** is the home of our "fight, flight, or freeze" instincts. This is the part of the brain in which our caveperson impulses live, the part that tells us we should seek shelter from the elements, avoid touching fire, and find food when our bellies are empty. In the modern era, those instincts are still laser-focused on survival. One of our most basic and primal human needs is the need to belong—if we're part of a group, we are safer and have a much better chance of survival. So our primitive brain is always automatically putting people, places, and things into categories. Will this person or thing help or hinder my survival? We often say we feel things in our gut, when in fact it's really our primitive brain weighing in. When facilitating, I sometimes get pushback on this idea: *Shouldn't I follow my gut instincts?* But if we called that instinct what it was, we'd probably think differently. When we're following our gut instincts, we're following our reptilian brain, the least evolved part of our brains, the part focused on whether or not we are going to die. These instincts are wired to focus us on avoiding threat and self-preservation, not on logical decision making and critical thinking.

The **emotional brain** houses memory and experience. It comes into the world as a blank slate and is programmed based on our values, beliefs, assumptions, and experiences. We often don't even think; we just respond out of our emotions. Problems arise when the programming doesn't serve us well or limits our ability to correctly interpret and fully engage with the world around us. The emotional brain helps us have empathy and feel connected to other people, but it can also make us irrational in our reactions to stimuli about which we have high emotion.

Finally, the **thinking brain** is where our higher-level processing, problem solving, and creativity occur. In many ways, this part of the brain separates humans from the rest of the animal world. We have the ability to step apart from our own values, beliefs, assumptions, and experiences. We can see the world through someone else's eyes. Interestingly, even when the thinking part of the brain is focused on higher-level processing, the primitive and emotional parts of our brains are still engaged, taking in information and doing their best to throw a wrench in the thinking brain if they feel threatened. When we find ourselves in certain circumstances, the power of those primitive and emotional parts of the brain, their overwhelming desire to keep us safe, can overtake the thinking brain and our ability to consciously process and act.

Bias Can Activate Our Primitive and Emotional Brain

Imagine this scenario. You're having a feedback conversation with your boss. She's carefully considered how she will frame this feedback, attended training on sensitive conversations, and read articles on effective feedback. She is operating in her thinking brain. The two of you sit down, and she begins to deliver the feedback.

Immediately after hearing the word "feedback," you feel your heartbeat accelerating. You have a disability that requires an accommodation, and recently your colleagues have been complaining that you're receiving special treatment. You're positive this "feedback" conversation is really an attempt to take away your accommodation. As your boss speaks, you think of all the ways you've been slighted before: the focus on your disability instead of on results, the lack of acknowledgment of your hard work. Sensing a threat, you are operating from the emotional or even primitive part of your brain. Before the conversation has even begun, you are operating from one part of your brain and your boss is operating from another.

> **MARK**
>
> I learned to speak Spanish fairly fluently when I lived in Argentina and now live in Texas, which has a large Hispanic population. I love every opportunity I can get to practice my Spanish.
>
> I was having lunch with some friends in San Antonio at a popular taquería—a great place to practice my Spanish, I thought. All of the staff was Hispanic. When I got to the counter to place my order, I decided to place it in Spanish, hoping it would be seen as respectfully engaging in her culture. Instead, to my surprise, she took great offense and said very curtly, "I do speak English, you know!" I quickly tried to clarify my intent, but the damage was done.
>
> It dawned on me that this must not have been the first time she had experienced something similar, and when she had, it must have been a negative experience for her. Who knows how many times her identity had been questioned in similar ways.

When bias—or even the threat of bias—triggers our brains in this way, we talk past each other, often making the situation worse instead of better, moving into the Limiting or Damaging Zone as opposed to the High-Performance Zone.

Psychological Safety

To avoid activating the emotional or primitive parts of our brains, we need to feel psychologically safe—secure in the sense that we are not under threat. Researchers define psychological safety in the workplace as "the belief that you won't be punished when you make a mistake."*

---

* Laura Delizonna, "High-Performing Teams Need Psychological Safety. Here's How to Create It." *Harvard Business Review,* August 24, 2017; https://hbr.org/2017/08/high-performing-teams-need-psychological-safety-heres-how-to-create-it.

That mistake can be anything from a technical error to saying or doing the wrong thing for the environment.

MARK

Some organizations proclaim to be open to making mistakes and "failing fast," but their practices and the experiences of their people tell a different story. I worked with a hospital that holds innovation as one of their core values. To this end, they engaged us to create and execute a development program designed to foster greater innovation.

I had a candid conversation with the client, who shared the challenges she foresaw in building competency around innovation. Principal among them was the fact that creating opportunities for innovation was limited because of the very cautious culture and intolerance for error or mistakes. In other words, there was very little psychological safety.

Subsequent conversations with several employees confirmed what she had told me. One employee said, "They tell us to be creative in our approach to problem solving. But if we try something new and the problem isn't resolved immediately and perfectly, we're reprimanded, sometimes publicly!" The organization's bias for avoiding risk overtook the need for innovation in daily practice.

For people to give their best efforts, they need to know they will be supported, even when they occasionally miss the mark.

The Equal Employment Opportunity Commission (EEOC), the federal agency responsible for preventing discrimination in U.S. workplaces, determined risk factors that make an environment more susceptible to harassment and discrimination. Those risk factors center around power dynamics: an "us versus them" dynamic that can show up between the field and headquarters; or when "the customer is always right" and employees aren't heard; or when organizations have only a few high-value employees. If I'm working with a star executive, how likely am I to bring up something problematic versus if I'm working with a peer? When power is imbalanced and allowed to remain that way, we're at greater risk of entering the Damaging Zone of the Performance Model. When an imbalance of power is present in the conversation, we do not feel psychologically safe. We are also more susceptible to behave with bias, or be on the receiving end of bias, depending on where we reside in that power dynamic. These ideas overlay one another—psychological safety allows us to be in the High-Performance Zone and increases the likelihood of our operating from the thinking part of our brains.

So how do we build psychological safety? How do we shift our decision-making processes from the emotional and primitive parts of the brain to the thinking brain? The answer lies in evening out the power dynamic. Each of us has formal and informal authority in conversations at work. Whether we are at the lower or the higher end of the power dynamic, we can habitually build circumstances around psychological safety. Consider the following as you work to establish psychological safety in your interactions with others, in particular with subordinates or those with less status in the organization:

- Are we in my office, your office, or a neutral third space?

- Are we both sitting or standing?

- If I feel emotional about an issue, have we communicated via email before the conversation to ensure our expectations are clear and we both have the information we need?

- Have I shared how important this issue is to me and why I take it personally?

- Is there someone else in the organization I should bring in to support a neutral starting point?

The Promise of Neuroplasticity

The *Harvard Business Review* conducted research on the efficacy of traditional unconscious bias and diversity training, and found that it was not effective when it was made mandatory. If you dig into the research, you'll see that one reason for this is that most unconscious bias training is focused specifically on devillainizing bias.*

If we learn only that bias is a natural part of how the brain works and are told that the cognitive shortcuts in our brains are unchangeable, we're absolved of that responsibility. *I have bias. I have certain preferences. Moving right along.* But that's far from the end of the story, thanks to neuroplasticity.

Neuroplasticity is the brain's ability to create lasting change at any age. We can use self-awareness to pause and examine whether or not our brains are acting from the primitive or emotional parts. We can assess the impact of that bias on ourselves and others. Then we can choose how to proceed. This process builds new neural pathways in your brain and becomes a habitual lens on our decision making.

ANNE

It's not easy to embrace self-awareness. Time pressures, our dependence on digital communications media, the dynamic nature of the world around us all might lull us into thinking, "It's okay. I can't pause or think about that now. Let's just forge ahead."

I have found that in order to embrace self-awareness, there are a couple of questions to consider:

- Give yourself a moment to reflect and ask yourself why. Why did I choose to say that? Why did I think that? Why did that person react in that way?

- What am I assuming? Are my assumptions based on fact or experiences, or on something less concrete? Furthermore, are they based on someone else's beliefs or experiences as opposed to my own?

---

* Edward H. Chang et al. "Does Diversity Training Work the Way It's Supposed To?" *Harvard Business Review,* July 9, 2019; https://hbr.org/2019/07/does-diversity-training-work-the-way-its-supposed-to.

> If the why is not clear, ask a trusted colleague. Depending on your role, you might not be getting the "real feedback." Ask for it. By doing so, you'll create an environment where it's safe to give and receive feedback.

We can leverage neuroplasticity to forge new pathways that help us mitigate negative bias. So while bias is a natural part of how the brain works, so is neuroplasticity. This means that when we manage to identify bias in our views, interactions, or decision making, we can take action. We can use the Performance Model to think through the result of that bias.

If the impact is negative, in the Limiting or Damaging Zone, we can lean into the brain's ability to create new habits to shift to high performance. The education bias I shared earlier is a good example of this. Based on the value I put on education, my brain used to go straight to education as I reviewed résumés. I consciously trained myself to look first at the person's most recent job. I'm now so accustomed to doing things this way that I sometimes need to go back to look at the education piece. Neuroplasticity ensures there is hope for us as we reframe how we think about bias and what we can do to have a positive impact.

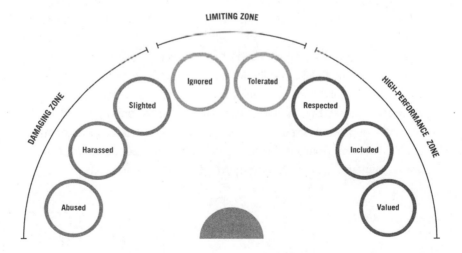

ANNE

According to Abraham Maslow's hierarchy of needs, safety is one of our foundational needs as humans. Many go to the obvious needs of physical safety, property safety, and health—but paramount in the pursuit of belonging, esteem, and potential is psychological safety. If people don't feel they are in a safe environment, a place where they can speak their minds, be respected for who they are, and trust in the integrity of the system and those around them, the full potential of the person, team, and organization will never be realized.

Think about this. Were you ever in an environment where you were afraid to speak up? Throughout the course of my career, I can't begin to count the number of times when I felt this way. Why and how does this happen? Looking back, I often felt too young, too inexperienced, too stupid, too junior, too different, too scared to suffer the consequences of having a dissenting point of view or too convinced it wasn't my place.

How does one overcome this self-limiting bias? The three most important steps are embracing your authenticity, leaning on others, and ensuring you're in an environment that brings out the best in you.

What is the role of the leader in creating a safe environment for teams and individuals to thrive? Great leaders are all about building a culture of integrity, trust, transparency, collaboration, and communication—where it's okay to fail. In these cultures, failure is viewed as an integral part of responsible risk-taking with a bias toward action and improvement. Leaders know that failure is simply learning on the pathway to success. Great leaders build an environment where continuous learning is paramount and where that learning comes from anyone, anywhere, at any time in, around, and across the organization. Coupled with a clear, compelling vision and purpose, these teams attract the best and most diverse talent and deliver the most innovative, sustainable results.

Chapter 2: Understand the Neuroscience
Reflection for Individuals

Different situations, people, or topics often trigger one of the three parts of our brains (primitive, emotional, and thinking). Because of this, conversations can quickly dissolve into frustration and conflict. Recognizing the neuroscience driving our reactions can help us identify what is happening and allow us to adjust our approach.

1. Recall a time when you had a conversation or an interaction that you believed was pragmatic and logical, but the person you were speaking with was becoming emotional. Describe what you observed about the other person—tone of voice, facial expressions, body movements, posture, language used. How did the conversation end?

....

....

....

....

2. Now think about a conversation where you felt strongly about something and the person you were speaking with seemed calculating or cold, unable to understand why this was so important to you. Describe what you observed about the other person—tone of voice, facial expressions, body movements, posture, and language used. How did the conversation end?

....

....

....

....

Chapter 2: Understand the Neuroscience
Application for Leaders

Building psychological safety is about balancing the scales of power in human interaction. While leaders and managers do have authority in the workplace, utilizing that power to dominate conversations can be damaging.

1. Consider these different components of power and the tips provided for each component before engaging in an important conversation:

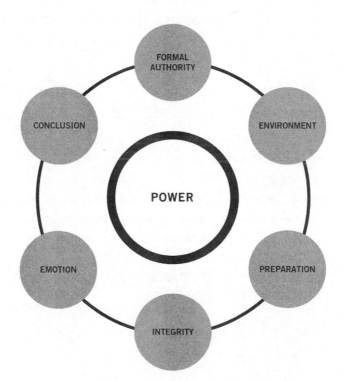

Formal Authority. Acknowledge your level of formal authority and be clear about what is possible in this conversation. For example, "This decision has already been made, and the reality is we will be proceeding in this direction. And I'd like to listen to your concerns so we can work through them together." Declaring your intent at the beginning of the conversation and setting the boundaries of what is possible ensures aligned expectations.

Environment. These are the physical realities of the conversation. Where are you having the conversation—my office, your office, or a neutral third space? Are you behind the desk? Is it a virtual meeting? Is it in private, or in a more public space? Consider what the environment reflects about the power dynamics at play.

Preparation. Surprise will immediately push a person into the primitive part of the brain. Fielding an unexpected inquiry or having to answer an unexpected question puts us in defensive mode. Create space between the topic and the other person's need to respond by sending a preliminary communication or allowing for follow-up meetings.

Integrity. Ensure you practice integrity and behave in a way that aligns with the intent you set up front. Are you interrupting? Are you listening empathically? Restate your intent and what you are hearing to ensure your actions are aligned with your words.

Emotion. Check your emotions and those of the other person. If voices are being raised or trembling, eyes are filling with tears, someone is standing up or gesturing more dramatically than they normally do, it's time to pause and finish the conversation at a later time. Give yourself (or the other person) the opportunity to shift back to the thinking brain.

Conclusion. Accountability is a big part of psychological safety. What do you both agree to do as a result of this conversation? Are you both comfortable with the outcome? Is a future conversation warranted to circle back on the issue?

2. Identify two or three important conversations you intend to have in the upcoming days or weeks. Think about how the conversations will affect the other person(s). Are they likely to go into the primitive, emotional, or thinking brain? Take time to plan the conversations beforehand, then rehearse them with a trusted colleague or friend. What can you say or do to create psychological safety?

....

....

....

....

....

....

....

....

....

....

....

....

....

....

....

....

....

....

Chapter 3: Recognize the Bias Traps

We can be blind to the obvious, and we are also blind to our blindness.

—Daniel Kahneman, Nobel Prize–winning economist and psychologist

Bias traps are circumstances in which we are more susceptible to lean into biased thinking. Understanding them ensures we can recognize and avoid them when necessary. Our brains are supercomputers, and they have a capacity problem. As we mentioned in the introduction, we are faced with about eleven million pieces of information every minute, but we can consciously process only about forty of them. Cognitive shortcuts allow us to handle the difference.

In a practical sense, if we had to think about every little step to some action like putting our pants on in the morning, we'd probably all still be in our pajamas. Part of that processing, that supercomputer work, is good. It helps us get through the world without paying attention to all eleven million bits of information.

If you've heard about types of biases before, you've probably heard terms like "confirmation bias," "negativity bias," or "halo effect." These are terms used for the specific biases our brains employ to come to conclusions. In fact, researchers have identified and defined more than 180 different kinds of biases or cognitive shortcuts. Reviewing all 180-plus biases would be an exercise in futility. You won't remember them all, and most of us aren't neuroscientists.

For the purpose of really being able to identify bias, let's talk about three traps that represent common circumstances when our brains are most susceptible to bias in the workplace, most susceptible to falling into one of the many possible biases: Information Overload, Feelings Over

Facts, and the Need for Speed. When we are in these circumstances, the brain pushes more information to the side in order to focus on the forty bits of information it can actively process. And in that process, our brains sometimes push aside important pieces of information. When you are overwhelmed, highly emotional, or rushed (for some of us, that's quite often), your brain is more likely to lean into the shortcuts.

Let's define each of these bias traps in more detail and align them to specific biases that can occur in each circumstance. As you read through these examples, we'd recommend pausing after each one and thinking of an example you've experienced or witnessed. As with all the skills in this section, draw on your ability to be self-aware and explore the possibilities.

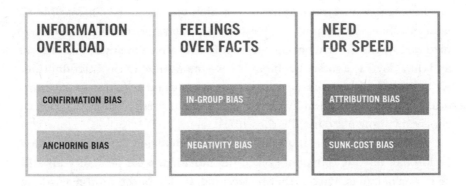

INFORMATION OVERLOAD	FEELINGS OVER FACTS	NEED FOR SPEED
CONFIRMATION BIAS	IN-GROUP BIAS	ATTRIBUTION BIAS
ANCHORING BIAS	NEGATIVITY BIAS	SUNK-COST BIAS

Information Overload

When we face an overwhelming amount of data or inputs, we're at risk of **Information Overload.** Our brains have learned to automatically filter much of that information, even the bits that might be useful. For example, if we have hundreds of résumés to plow through, we might be more likely to lean into bias to help us make fast assessments. Two examples of cognitive shortcuts that occur in Information Overload are confirmation bias and anchoring bias.

Confirmation bias is the idea that we tend to seek information that supports our existing beliefs. It's a way to filter and focus. For example, when we want to catch up on the news, we don't watch all available outlets and we rarely do our own investigative reporting. As we mentioned in Chapter 1, we usually watch the news outlet that supports our political leanings in order to hear perspectives that align with our own. Or at work, perhaps a manager is on the team evaluating new IT systems or a new piece of equipment for a manufacturing operation. She advocates heavily for System A over System B. Three months into the implementation, she has aggregated fifteen examples of why this was the better choice, while the rest of the committee is hearing significant feedback that the system is not working. She is seeking out only the information that confirms System A, the system she believes to be superior.

Interestingly, research suggests "people experience genuine pleasure—a rush of dopamine—when processing information that supports their beliefs." Psychiatrist Jack Gorman writes: "It feels good to 'stick to our guns' even if we are wrong."*

Anchoring bias is the idea that we rely on the first piece of information we see to make decisions. Say your design team presents three options for a new logo. Anchoring bias means we'll have an automatic preference for the first one we see, regardless of its actual value.

Anchoring bias is evident in first impressions. We make a multitude of judgments about people's character, intellect, ability, and so forth within the first few minutes—or even seconds—of meeting them. If we think back to the iceberg, we know that there's more to each of us than a first impression can capture. But once those biases are there, they can be awfully hard to replace.

Have you seen these biases show up in your workplace or even in your own leadership style? And for that matter, in your relationships outside of work?

Feelings Over Facts

Many of us would say that our beliefs are factual (we see this a lot in heated debates!).

But of course, our perceptions are not always accurate. Picture in your mind how large you believe the United States is geographically

---

* Sara E. Gorman and Jack Gorman, *Denying to the Grave: Why We Ignore the Facts That Will Save Us*. UK: Oxford University Press, 2016.

compared to Africa. Think about maps you've seen. Is it significantly larger? About the same size? Minuscule? Now picture China, India, and the United Kingdom. How big are they? China and India have some of the highest population densities in the world. Then check out the accurate map on page 52. It not only compares these countries to the continent of Africa, but literally fits them inside. How correct were your perceptions?

Most people drastically underestimate the geographical size of Africa, because how we *feel* about a continent's prominence in the world overweighs the facts. This feeling is admittedly driven by what we've been exposed to in the past. For Americans, we learn about history and politics and culture through the lens of America and with America at the center—the most prominent, if you will. This is true of most countries and continents.

As our brains absorb information, the emotional and primitive parts preempt the thinking part and turn our beliefs about that information into facts. We discussed this in Chapter 2, when research participants couldn't solve math problems if the answer would conflict with their political beliefs. In the absence of information, our brains fill in the blanks, often by drawing on how we feel about a situation. We then operate as if it is fact.

ANNE

To feel is to be human. We don't want to suppress our feelings; after all, progressive, contemporary leaders are known to be empathic, humble, authentic, and caring.

However, we must realize our feelings can also be the source of bias. We're wired to desire connections with others. Hence, it's natural that each one of us gravitates toward those with whom we share some background, whether it's a common alma mater, ethnicity, gender, religion, or company. When we're identifying high-potential leaders, giving performance ratings or feedback, or making financial decisions for our team members, we need to be vigilant in ensuring that our feelings and biases don't cloud a more holistic, balanced view of the situation. How? Every one of us needs trusted advisors in the workplace. Whether it's your human resources partners, your legal team, or a peer, it's important to bounce decisions off others who will likely have a different point of view. In my experience, I've found that having structured calibration discussions in the form of 1-on-1 check-ins, especially with those whom you may spend less time with on a day-to-day basis, in combination with ad hoc "Do you have a couple of minutes to talk?" sessions works best for me. And note—it's talk . . . not text, email, chat, or otherwise. Talking live with someone enables authentic interaction, reaction, emotion, perspective, and connection in ways that are not replaceable by other digital forms.

So how does this bias trap of feelings over facts come about in common biases we might hold? Two common biases are in-group bias and negativity bias.

In-group bias is our tendency to favor people we like or those who are like us, while excluding those who are different. Say I'm a leader assigned a new project, and I'm told I get to pick my team from the rest of my colleagues. In-group bias means I'll unconsciously tend to pick people who act like me, agree with me, or look like me. There's another introvert on the team, so I pick him. There's a woman on the team, so I pick her. There's another Latina on the team, so I pick her. This is comfortable, but it doesn't lead to the best results. In-group bias can be especially insidious in hiring practices, team assignments, and customer engagement.

A recent study highlighted another example of in-group bias by finding 71 percent of leaders selected protégés of the same race and gender.[*] The tendency to seek similarity as a guideline for mentorship and coaching can have a significant impact on the leadership pipeline and succession planning within an organization.

MARK

I worked with a client who realized that in-group bias was negatively affecting important projects. Traditionally, "important" projects were given to people with tenure, because the bias was that experienced people would have the most insight. To combat this, they mandated

---

[*] The Sponsor Dividend, Center for Talent Innovation, 2019; https://www.talent innovation.org/publication.cfm?publication=1640.

that when certain projects reached the threshold of truly "important," they had to include at least one project team member with less than six months in the organization. They subsequently learned that much of the most innovative thinking was coming from the new hire who didn't know how things were "supposed" to be done. A fresh set of eyes provided a significant benefit. In fact, research has found that the presence of "socially distinct newcomers" can stimulate new thinking and more breakthroughs in a group.*

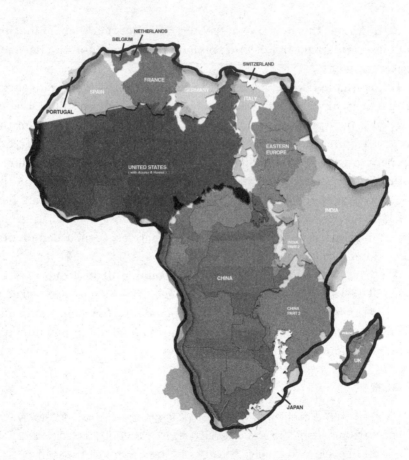

---

* Katherine W. Phillips, Katie A. Liljenquist, and Margaret A. Neale, "Is the Pain Worth the Gain? The Advantages and Liabilities of Agreeing with Socially Distinct Newcomers." *Personality and Social Psychology Bulletin* 35, no. 3 (2009); https://doi.org/10.1177/0146167208328062.

Negativity bias is when we are more powerfully affected by negative experiences than positive ones. Think back to when you were a kid. You probably remember when you were grounded more vividly than all the times you weren't in trouble. We and others hold on to the negative experience, not the full picture. In a sales context, you might consistently hit your goals quarter after quarter. But if you miss a quarter, it tends to affect your reputation. We hold on to that single negative outcome instead of the many positive ones that preceded it.

Similarly, we might work with a team member who is significantly different from us. Perhaps they speak with an accent, serve in a different job function, or lack a credential we have. Let's say we've worked with this person before without any problems. Then they make an error. Negativity bias would be present if we held on to their error to the exclusion of all their successes. We might even extend it to the person's identity—for example, "This never would have happened if someone older was in charge," or "This really needed to be done by someone in finance."

ANNE

The power of negativity bias is profound in a world that's digitally connected through numerous forms of social media and we have access to information in real time. Think about your buying behavior today, whether it's your assessment as to which brand of product or service to buy or even your decision about what new restaurant to try. We are now trained to seek the feedback, views, and ratings of others—most of whom are total strangers! A negative rating might mean we don't even give a restaurant, product, or brand a chance.

Negativity bias in the workplace is particularly powerful if we've experienced it ourselves. I recall a time when I made a key staffing decision that was risky at the outset—bringing in someone from sales who had only been in the field into a critical staff role. It was a bomb. Fault can be attributed to all involved, including me. I'll admit that this experience clouded my point of view going forward. Even though the employee had been competent in their prior role and this new role just wasn't a good fit, the negative aspects of the experience made me reluctant to take the same risk again. For a period of time after that staffing failure, I had to consciously check myself for not assuming another person with a similar background wouldn't be successful in a similar circumstance. To counter negativity bias, you need to recognize that no two situations are exactly the same, realizing that there are always underlying factors (often unseen) also at play.

MARK

In my role as a senior consultant, my participants often fill out evaluations at the end of a work session to measure initial impact. In a class of twenty-five people, I might get twenty-four glowing positive evaluations, but I inevitably obsess over the single negative comment. Clients do the same with 360-degree feedback and annual performance reviews. That's negativity bias in action! You'll often hear that building a culture of coaching and feedback is integral to employee engagement and performance. But this instinct, negativity bias, which we can fall into when we have high emotions about the data (Feelings Over Facts), is one of the things that gets in the way.

The Need for Speed

The **Need for Speed** occurs when we cut corners to act quickly. Often these time-savers are based on bias and can be simplistic, self-centered, and even counterproductive.

Some of the Need for Speed is born from survival instincts, the primitive brain, or the idea of "fight or flight or freeze" instinctual reaction. But the Need for Speed can also come into play organizationally and can result in snap judgments, bias, and misperceptions. We need to fill a position immediately, so we hire a colleague's niece instead of completing a competitive hiring process. Our article is due this afternoon, so we make some critical assumptions instead of running down sources and completing interviews based on fact. A client is angry, and we dismiss them as difficult so we can get through the customer service queue, rather than slowing down and getting to the root of the problem.

MARK

This bias trap, the Need for Speed, can also hamper a leader's ability to coach to performance or delegate. The transition from individual contributor to a leader who achieves results through others is fraught with this conundrum: "I can do it faster and better myself right now, or I can slow down and spend the time to train my team to do it faster and better time and time again in the future." When we fall into the Need for Speed, we default to the first option; it takes less time in the moment but is inefficient in the long term. As we say in our senior leader program, *The 4 Essential Roles of Leadership,* "Telling creates dependency; coaching creates capability."

Two common biases under the Need for Speed are attribution bias and sunk-cost bias. **Attribution bias** is the idea that we judge others on their actions, but we judge ourselves on our intent. If I make a mistake, I have a very good explanation for it and I know my intent was good. If colleagues make a mistake, they're fundamentally flawed—disorganized, cavalier, or uncommitted. Stated differently, we give ourselves the benefit of the doubt and the additional time to make a contribution and don't naturally extend that benefit to others. As Stephen M. R. Covey, bestselling author of *The Speed of Trust,* says, "We tend to judge ourselves by our intentions, and others by their observable behavior."

Consider team dynamics. Suppose you have a new team member in a role you used to do. He takes much longer to submit a report than you did when you were in that role. You start to believe he's a fundamentally slow worker, ignoring the fact that you were in that role much longer than he's been. And in circumstances like these, that attribution can even be extended to identifiers the person has, like generation, ethnicity, or job function.

Sunk-cost bias is our tendency to continue our current course of action because we've invested time, money, or energy into it. It's the idea that we have reached a point of no return. This bias can show up in our personal life when we have a hard time letting go of expensive possessions, even after they've outlived their usefulness. It shows up many ways professionally as well—from the process we can't see past because "that's the way we've always done it," to the failing projects we continue to dump time and money into because our egos are overly invested in this being the "best" idea.

ANNE

For organizations, teams, and individuals who have significant tenure, sunk-cost bias can be particularly damaging. While experience is valuable, sometimes it can work to one's detriment. A comment such as "We've already committed to doing it this way, and it's too late to change course" is a sign that sunk-cost bias is at play.

In this dynamic marketplace where the speed of innovation, change, and transformation is only accelerating, I often bring up the old adage that "What got us here won't get us there." The bar continues to be raised—by customers, by competitors, by macro forces at large such as the economy and the regulatory environment—and what success looks like continues to evolve. Bias can cause us to miss these external signals and fail to be proactive.

Chapter 3: Recognize the Bias Traps
Reflection for Individuals

The bias traps are Information Overload, Feelings Over Facts and the Need for Speed. When we are in these circumstances, we are overwhelmed, rely on the pull of our emotions over what we know to be fact, and succumb to the impulse of shortcuts in order to act quickly. The best strategy for not falling into bias traps is to build your awareness of them, create space to hijack those instincts, then take control of your decision-making process. Under each bias trap, we have outlined two examples of the specific biases we can fall into when we are in each circumstance. Meaning, when we are in information overload, we are susceptible to confirmation and anchoring bias.

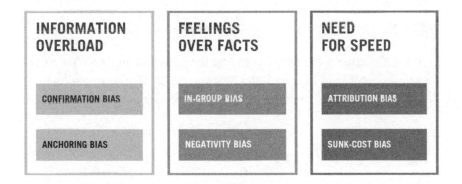

INFORMATION OVERLOAD	FEELINGS OVER FACTS	NEED FOR SPEED
CONFIRMATION BIAS	IN-GROUP BIAS	ATTRIBUTION BIAS
ANCHORING BIAS	NEGATIVITY BIAS	SUNK-COST BIAS

Choose one of the above bias traps to further explore, being mindful of the two sample biases that show up within that particular trap:

- Confirmation bias (seeing only information that supports an existing belief).

- Anchoring bias (relying on the first piece of information to make a decision).

- In-group bias (favoring people we like or those who are like us).

- Negativity bias (being more affected by negative instead of positive experiences).

- Attribution bias (giving ourselves the benefit of the doubt and not extending that courtesy to others).

- Sunk-cost bias (resisting the need to change course due to all that has already been invested).

Avoiding the Trap

1. Select a bias trap you might be prone to fall into. Increase your self-awareness by listing how, where, when, and what triggers this bias trap for you.

....

....

....

2. What are actions you can take to create space and hit pause between what triggers your bias trap and how you react? (For example, taking a break from social media's "echo chamber" can help with confirmation bias.)

....

....

....

3. Take control of your decision making by evaluating the costs (and potential benefits) of your bias in action. Consider the steps you can take to mitigate, avoid, or better control your bias trap. Make a list of the behaviors you can stop, modify, or do more of.

....

....

....

Chapter 3: Recognize the Bias Traps
Application for Leaders

For leaders, a second level of questioning reveals the organizational impact of the three bias traps.

1. As a leader, you're making decisions of significant magnitude on a daily basis. Pausing to assess the *impact* of those decisions can ensure you aren't falling into the bias traps as you make them. Assess the impact by answering the following:

   • Does the decision impact someone's professional opportunity or future growth?

   ....

   ....

   ....

   • Does it have large financial repercussions for you or the business?

   ....

   ....

   ....

   • Is it a change that will impact other people or the business?

   ....

   ....

   ....

- Is it valuable but perhaps not critical to achieving results?

....

....

....

2. If the answer to any of these questions is yes, pause and create space between yourself and the decision or interaction by:

- Seeking perspective from a trusted colleague or friend before making the decision.

....

....

....

- Taking notes on both sides of the decision: make yourself argue for the opposite perspective.

....

....

....

- Sleeping on it, if you can. By waiting until the next day, you're literally creating space between your emotions and the decision.

....

....

....

....

....

Chapter 4: Embrace Mindfulness

Almost everything will work again if you unplug it for a few minutes. Including you.[*]

—Anne Lamott, bestselling author of *Bird by Bird*

Some people dismiss mindfulness as not sophisticated or "hard edged" enough to be a leadership skill. They think the word is limited to an ashram in a far flung destination or reserved for times of extreme relaxation. But mindfulness is one of the most critical skills required to identify bias in ourselves and others. Our minds are incredibly prone to wandering away from what's happening in the present moment; we spend almost half of our day thinking about something other than what we're actually doing.[†] Without mindfulness, decisions become automatic. We often categorize people in binary terms like good or bad, important or unimportant, adding value or wasting time, right or wrong.

So, what is mindfulness, and how do we use it to mitigate bias? Mindfulness is a state of mind achieved by concentrating our awareness on the present moment, focusing on our feelings, thoughts, and senses to better understand how we engage with others and react to stimuli.

Researchers Christina Congleton, Britta Hölzel, and Sara Lazar

---

[*] Anne Lamott, "12 Truths I Learned from Life and Writing." TED talk, April 2017; https://www.ted.com/talks/anne_lamott_12_truths_i_learned_from_life_and_writing.

[†] Matthew A. Killingsworth and Daniel T. Gilbert, "A Wandering Mind Is an Unhappy Mind." *Science* 330, no. 6006 (November 12, 2010), 932; doi: 10.1126/science.1192439.

write: "Mindfulness should no longer be considered a 'nice to have' for executives. It's a 'must have': a way to keep our brains healthy, to support self-regulation and effective decision-making capabilities, and to protect ourselves from toxic stress," all of which can impact our ability to discern and act on unconscious bias.*

Ultimately, we're trying to create the pause between information coming in and our emotional reactions to that information. As we've already established, our brains are supercomputers, and the brain's automatic programming impacts decisions both big and small. Developing a mindfulness practice can mitigate potential negative impacts of bias. For example, I'm left-handed, which means when I facilitate with clients, I unconsciously have a bias toward the left side of the room and unintentionally give more attention to those learners. Being mindful has helped me intentionally use the full presentation space when delivering. I can move to the other side of the room to make a point, give instructions, or ask for opinions on a concept. This is something small, but it can make a difference in whether others are drawn into the conversation or whether they feel excluded by my body language.

A strong mindfulness practice helps us become more conscious of our own thoughts and feelings. In my experience, many of us describe ourselves as self-aware, but the fact is, we really aren't—me included. We all know leaders who say they're open to people's ideas, then shut down every idea that isn't their own. Sometimes that lack of self-awareness is more subtle, as when someone blames a system for a bias they might have: "I'm very committed to diversity; we just can't find candidates that meet the qualifications." (For the record, there are qualified, diverse candidates for just about every role, although finding them may require us to recruit in new and different ways.) Self-awareness is not easy; it requires serious introspection, which journalist Chris Hayes described as an intellectual pursuit, the heavy lifting of looking inside yourself and sorting out what you find. This is challenging, but as is

---

* Christina Congleton, Britta K. Hölzel, and Sara W. Lazar, "Mindfulness Can Literally Change Your Brain." *Harvard Business Review,* January 8, 2015; https://hbr.org/2015/01/mindfulness-can-literally-change-your-brain.

true of any skill, we can improve it with practice. This is the essence of neuroplasticity.

Strategies to Strengthen Your Mindfulness Muscles

My son has a card game called Mindfulness Matters: The Game That Uses Mindfulness Skills to Improve Coping in Everyday Life. It builds mindfulness, observation, and awareness skills. You divvy out the cards, then take turns completing a mindfulness activity, like: "Use objects in the room to tell a story." We use this game because of my son's neurodiversity. Over the course of his elementary school career, my son has been diagnosed with ADHD and traits associated with the autism spectrum. The term "neurodiversity" is being used more commonly to define "the idea that neurological differences like autism and ADHD are the result of normal, natural variation in the human genome."[*] Instead of looking at these disabilities as a hindrance, the medical community and organizations and workplaces globally are recognizing the advantage of engaging with problems and ideas through this different lens. Neurodiversity is a growing focus of inclusion programs.

While my son's neurodiversity is an advantage in his critical thinking and problem-solving skills, as his parents, my husband and I have to be proactive in building his muscles around responding to social cues and collaborating with others. The more I play these games with him, the more I realize I don't know how to practice mindfulness that well either—and neither do most adults!

An effective mindfulness practice, one that is robust and can be maintained, is unique to the individual. Mine won't look like yours, and yours won't look like anyone else's. It can be hard to know where to start, so we've outlined some best practices below. Consider it an array of starting points you can try as you see fit.

---

[*] Robert D. Austin and Gary P. Pisano, "Neurodiversity as a Competitive Advantage." *Harvard Business Review,* May–June 2017; https://hbr.org/2017/05/neurodiversi ty-as-a-competitive-advantage.

Build a Regular Meditation Practice

As compared to non-meditators, those who meditate are better at self-regulating their thoughts and emotions and focusing on a goal while resisting distractions; they generally perform better on tasks that require sustained attention.[*] If sitting on a meditation cushion doesn't appeal to you, don't give up yet: the *Cambridge Dictionary* defines meditation as "the act of giving your attention to only one thing, either as a religious activity or as a way of becoming calm and relaxed," or "serious thought or study, or the product of this activity." So meditation can include relaxing, focusing, pondering, thinking, etc.

Meditation can be done in just a few moments or last much longer. Apps and podcasts can walk you through a guided meditation from beginner to advanced, in many different styles. Just keep experimenting until you find one that appeals to you.

ANNE

As I've gotten older, I've come to value and prioritize my health. I've also come to realize that my mental and emotional health are directly correlated to my physical health. Thus, my ability to be mindful is absolutely tied to my physical well-being. After hitting a milestone birthday, I realized I was not at my best. My career was going great by all external measures, but I had lost myself. My stress level was at an all-time high and I felt down. The root cause was that I wasn't taking care of myself: mind, body, and soul. I was letting the voices in my head overcome me, and negative thoughts about myself began to shape my identity. The milestone birthday served as a catalyst for me to get myself back on track.

That year I discovered a new passion: fitness boxing. While boxing provides the best cardio I've ever experienced, an unintended benefit for me is that I discovered the power of mindfulness and being in the mo-

---

[*] P. A. van den Hurk et al., "Greater Efficiency in Attentional Processing Related to Mindfulness Meditation," *Quarterly Journal of Experimental Psychology* 63, no. 6 (June 2010): 1168–80; doi: 10.1080/17470210903249365.

ment. To do boxing classes well, you must stay unwaveringly focused on what you are doing. The mental focus coupled with the emotional release and the physical exertion have served as a welcome reboot for me, and without question, it has helped me develop a much more intentional approach to mindfulness. I realized that sometimes you just have to let go to be mindful. And if you don't find outlets—whether they be mental, emotional, or physical (or in my case, all of the above)—the distractions and tensions will work together to take you away from the moment and from being fully present.

Find something that centers you.

Pause and Describe

Have you ever had a "meeting after the meeting" with a colleague, described something that happened, and had that person counter your version of the event at every turn? For example, I might leave a meeting and say, "Did you hear Kate's tone in that meeting? She was clearly upset that my project was greenlit and hers was not." And my colleague might respond, "I think she was disappointed that her project didn't get approved, but she also said she was excited for you and eager to partner on next steps. Did you hear that part?" We were too busy creating a narrative in our minds to see what was actually happening.

When you're in a meeting or situation, take a moment to get out of your head and pay attention to the details around you. Are people engaged? What are their facial expressions? What tone of voice are they speaking in? You might even focus on concrete details like the color of the shirt they are wearing or what they're using to write, just to practice focusing. (As a bonus step, try watching the TV shows *Elementary* and *The Mentalist* to see this power of observation in action!)

Try a Tech Blackout

Most smartphones give you the ability to monitor how much you use your phone and for what purpose—mine tells me how much time I spend on productivity, social media, reading, or exercising. The newest version of Microsoft Outlook will send you a monthly wellness report highlighting how many days of the last thirty you shut down your email after traditional working hours. These apps and analytics help us set a goal for decreasing our reliance on technology, specifically the times that hurt our focus. Take a look at these analytics, then consider reducing your use of these apps or devices for certain times each day. People are often amazed by what they notice about the outside world when they're intentional about their use of technology.

MARK

I have a core group of friends that go to dinner at least once a month. We have instituted what we've lovingly dubbed the "Dallas Stack." At the beginning of dinner, we all put our cell phones in the middle of the table, and they stay there until the bill has been paid. If anyone gets their phone for any reason before the bill arrives, they pay the tab for the entire table. We're much more present in the conversation when the tech is stowed away. You can use this same strategy around a conference table. In that case, there's no bill to pay, but perhaps a friendly competition in another way can encourage positive behavior.

Technology, as we all know, has an incredible ability to hijack our attention to the detriment of our focus and relationships. Our smartphones may be one of our greatest obstacles to mindfulness. As my colleague and FranklinCovey's productivity expert Kory Kogon says, "Transcend your natural impulse to respond to every beep and buzz, and instead consciously act from a centered, clear-thinking perspective."

Preplan

We often skate through our day, reacting to whatever urgencies come up. This makes us more susceptible to bias due to the need for speed. As our colleague and author Victoria Roos Olsson wrote in *Everyone Deserves a Great Manager*: "It sounds counterintuitive to spend more time on planning if you're already so busy you can't even get your most important work done. But if you don't plan your week, you're at the mercy of the winds of change, reacting to what comes your way instead of deciding what's important and what you want to accomplish." We'd add that you'd be at the mercy of the bias traps as well. Preplanning ensures that you can build time into your day for thinking and processing. You won't go into a critical meeting feeling highly emotional about the meeting immediately preceding it because you would have built in thirty minutes to process the earlier meeting and prepare for the one ahead.

Take a few minutes before your day begins to jot down one or two priorities, then schedule them into your day. Be sure to include prep time and breaks in your schedule so you don't overbook yourself. You might find it useful to write down what you *won't* do that day so you can focus on your priorities. Heidi Grant Halvorson of Columbia University says, "When people engage in the right kind of planning, their success rate goes up on average between 200 and 300 percent."[*]

Zoom Out to the Big Picture

MARK

We sometimes get so consumed by the details that we miss the larger point or picture. When we are focused on individual steps, we might miss the final destination altogether. Another way to phrase this is to think about patterns instead of individual events. Unconscious bias can be so entrenched that a single data point might not unearth it—like a single difficult conversation, or an off-color comment that doesn't sit right, or a probing question that feels accusatory—but a pattern of that behavior, a zoomed-out view of that employee's experience, can tell a more substantive story as it relates to bias. We can practice this zooming out in all kinds of contexts. When I certify facilitators to teach our content, I emphasize that it's important not to focus on memorizing the entire facilitator guide, but instead to know the wider arc of the story you want to tell, with the associated transitions from slide to slide. Understand the end in mind or the bigger picture, then fill in with the detail. That way, we can stay mindful and focus more on the conversation happening in the moment versus the technical accuracy of every word we say.

---

[*] Heidi Grant Halvorson, *9 Things Successful People Do Differently.* Brighton, MA: Harvard Business Review Press, 2012.

Set Intention

To deal with bias, the solution can be as simple as priming the pump. Bring the unconscious to consciousness by setting an intention around mitigating bias. We can increase the likelihood of greater self-awareness through what we say, think, and do before an interaction or decision. For example, the NBA discovered that their referees were making disproportionately more calls against players of races other than their own. Surprisingly, the problem didn't require major or costly intervention. By simply bringing this issue to the referees' attention, the impact of the unconscious racial bias seemed to dissipate. As written in *Time,* "Yes, there was an issue with implicit bias in the past. And yes, this is understandable since implicit bias is fairly common. But after the issue was publicized, it appears the bias vanished. And that is good news for everyone since it suggests that implicit bias—which, as noted, is an unconscious bias—can be overcome if a person is aware that they have this bias."*

Consider before your next call, interview, or negotiation thinking about how you're feeling and resolve to remain in the thinking part of your brain. For example, before you review résumés, you might say, "I'm not going to make assumptions based on people's names." To a certain extent, you can clear away unconscious interferences with intention.

As you try these practices, they become second nature; they become habit. The automatic workings of our brains as they relate to bias can be problematic—when we leave them to chance. Building an intentional mindfulness practice creates a positive automatic process to counteract negative automatic processes, allowing us to better self-regulate. We won't react instinctively to emotions, and we'll be more effective in our decision making. We can better see the entire landscape and are not restricted to a myopic view, one that might be convenient or comfortable.

---

* David Berri, "What NBA Referees Can Teach Us About Overcoming Prejudices." *Time,* December 16, 2014; https://time.com/3635839/implicit-bias-nba-referees/.

Chapter 4: Embrace Mindfulness
Reflection for Individuals

Habits take time to build. While you explore the best way to build your mindfulness practice, commit to alternate between the following two practices each day:

Press Reset

Each day our biases and habits inform thousands of decisions we make. In a study from Cornell University, scientists estimated that we make approximately 221 decisions each day just about food. It can be hard to recognize the decision in the moment. But reflecting on the decisions we make each day can help provide clarity on our biases and habits.

1. Spend five minutes each day reflecting on your decisions, conversations, and actions. What did you do today that might have been influenced by bias, habits, or incorrect paradigms? What could you do differently tomorrow? Consider setting a recurring reminder in your work calendar to do this at the end of each day.

Catch Yourself

Metacognition is thinking about our own thinking. It's a vital skill for changing biases and habits. And it comes more easily with practice and effort.

2. Focus on unkind thoughts first. When they happen, pause and reflect on your own thinking. Did you have unkind thoughts about yourself or about others? Was the thought based on facts? Or was it based on an unrelated experience or habit? Can you learn more about the situation before you make any decisions or take action?

Chapter 4: Embrace Mindfulness
Application for Leaders

Create the space on your team for mindfulness with these strategies. Jot down some notes about how you might do each of these things:

- Spend the first fifteen minutes of a team meeting sharing your mindfulness practice and encouraging your team to consider how they could build mindfulness into their daily life. Ask them to rotate sharing a mindfulness practice ("Mindfulness Minute," if you will) at the start of a weekly meeting.

....

....

....

....

- Provide formal training for your team. Dedicating time and resources to building a mindfulness practice tells your team this is important and gives them skills to implement immediately. Asking them to figure it out on their own likely won't work.

....

....

....

....

- As you delegate tasks or launch new projects, think about how you can create space between notice and action. For example, do you announce at the team meeting that you're embarking on a new project and then dive right in? Or do you announce the project and then give people time to process the idea before moving forward?

....

....

....

....

....

....

....

....

....

....

....

....

....

....

....

....

....

....

That's where peace begins—not just in the plans of leaders, but in the hearts of people. Not just in some carefully designed process, but in the daily connections.*

—Barack Obama, former U.S. president

* Barack Obama, "Remarks of President Barack Obama to the People of Israel," the White House, U.S. Government, March 21, 2013. https://obamawhitehouse.archives.gov/the-press-office/2013/03/21/remarks-president-barack-obama-people-israel.

Part 2: Cultivate Connection

By intentionally building connection with others, we are essentially filling in the gaps in our supercomputer brains, leaving less room for assumptions and more room for human complexity and nuance.

In this section, we'll learn how to break through to better performance by connecting with and understanding others' points of view, which helps us explore, revise, or even change our own points of view.

When we cultivate connection with people through empathy and curiosity, we shift ourselves and those we engage with into the High-Performance Zone. Making connection can seem like fluff, something there just isn't time for. But cultivating connection *can* be done meaningfully and in a surprisingly short amount of time.

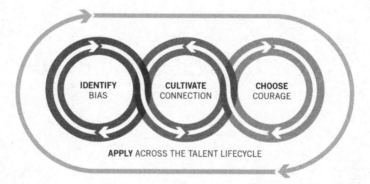

Frame/Reframe

Frame:	Reframe:
If I understand my biases, I can fix them on my own.	Only when I cultivate meaningful connections can I see past bias and value the people around me.

You may have heard the expression "The fish is the last to discover water." We can't see our own biases when we're surrounded by them. When we demonstrate empathy toward others, we're suspending our own beliefs, agendas, and interests in an effort to understand those of others. We make space for real breakthroughs to occur.

The Principle of Openness

When we are open with people, especially those who see the world differently than we do, *we* start seeing things differently, and this helps us see past our own biases. Being open requires vulnerability, a sentiment that goes against our naturally protective instincts. Engaging the emotional part of our brains to be open, vulnerable, and to build connection can help us move beyond these instinctual responses and shift to the High-Performance Zone.

So how do we build meaningful and substantive connection that can lead to breakthroughs? We start by focusing on belonging and our authentic selves, deploying empathy and curiosity intentionally, then tapping into the power of networks and effectively navigating difficult conversations about bias to get to understanding.

Chapter 5: Focus on Belonging

I am speaking to you as I always have—as the sober and serious man I have always wanted you to be, who does not apologize for his human feelings, who does not make excuses for his height, his long arms, his beautiful smile. You are growing into consciousness, and my wish for you is that you feel no need to constrict yourself to make other people comfortable. None of that can change the math anyway. I never wanted you to be twice as good as them, so much as I have always wanted you to attack every day of your brief bright life in struggle. . . . I would have you be a conscious citizen of this terrible and beautiful world.

—Ta-Nehisi Coates, National Book Award–winning author*

Cultivating connection is a two-sided endeavor. It involves the skill of building connection with others and also the value of knowing that others are cultivating connection with you. Ultimately, both sides of this enterprise impact performance.

Have you ever been somewhere and felt the need to make yourself fit in? Haven't we all felt this way to some degree? Middle school is infamous for being a time when no one fits—when our bodies outpace our maturity and often our age, when we are all awkward but also not quite mature enough to be kind to one another. For many of us, our middle school years are not a time we reflect on fondly. It is a period when our brains are working desperately to feel understood and connected to those around us. It's hard to recognize in the moment, but if you've spent time with a middle

---

* Ta-Nehisi Coates, *Between the World and Me*, New York: One World, 2015.

schooler since, you know this desire to belong leads to some real challenges in performance. The same can be said of adults in the workplace.

This internal desire doesn't actually change with age. Our brains are constantly trying to figure out whether we belong. Most researchers believe the need to belong is a critical psychological need. If we think about that primitive brain and the circumstances under which it developed, this makes sense. Are you more likely to be safe when you're alone, or when you're part of a group? Is it even possible to meet those psychological needs in isolation? We saw an extreme case of this in Tom Hanks's film *Cast Away*. The main character, stranded on an island, contrived a relationship with a volleyball, Wilson, to maintain some semblance of sanity, to meet his psychological needs.

And yet, in so many ways, our workplace structures don't cultivate belonging or promote connection. How often have you heard people use the word "fit" at work? We interview candidates and say they don't "fit," or someone quits and we say, "It's for the best; they didn't fit anyway." We put the onus on people to mold themselves into what we need or are comfortable with, instead of building work environments where people can naturally thrive. Many organizations have mastered building talent in their own likeness instead of allowing their people to utilize their unique talents and perspectives.

How We Came to Value Belonging

We've already defined bias, but other words will be relevant as we move through this topic. Let's begin with the basics: what is diversity and what is inclusion? "Diversity and inclusion" are often stated as if they're one word, but they're more akin to a doubles partnership in tennis—they're each distinct in approach and ability and, of course, they're better together. **Diversity** is about identity and representation, the composition of a workforce. The term "representation" is about parity; if you were to look at the U.S. Census and the percentages of race, national origin, gender, disability, veteran status, and other societal markers, does the workforce mirror those numbers? Is society represented in the organization's workforce? **Inclusion** is the idea that instead of needing to fit into a culture, people can bring their differing perspectives and opinions to the larger group without fear of rejection. Vernā Myers, vice president of inclusion strategy at Netflix and and founder of the Vernā Myers Company, states it this way: "Diversity is being invited to the party; inclusion is being asked to dance."

Three other words have recently appeared in the diversity and inclusion conversation: belonging, engagement, and equity. **Belonging** is a human need, just like the need for food and shelter. Consider what it feels like to be unwelcome. You walk into a room and the conversation stops, or you speak up in a meeting and your boss dismisses your idea. Getting to a place of belonging, where everyone can contribute their best, is the ultimate goal of diversity and inclusion.

Engagement is ultimately about empowerment, being asked for your opinion. Simply telling people they can speak up is different from shifting the power dynamic and inviting them to speak, sincerely saying, "I want your thoughts on this idea," or "I need your perspective on this problem." It is not just being encouraged or asked, but actually being listened to.

Equity is about bridging the opportunity gap. Talking about equity can feel uncomfortable, due to the stratification in society that results in some people having more opportunity than others. These opportunities sometimes result from a bias in favor of a desirable trait. Think about how we associate height with power, or how attractive people are spoken to more often than unattractive people (it starts when we're babies!). Sometimes these opportunities are affected by geography, like the enrichment activities I could access as a teenager in New York City in contrast to my peers in rural environments, or the number of free museums in Washington, D.C., as opposed to fee-charging museums in other parts of the world. And sometimes these opportunities are related to weightier characteristics like race, gender, national origin, and socioeconomics. For example, Hasan Minhaj, the host of *Patriot Act,* a weekly comedy show on Netflix, characterized graduating from college with debilitating student-loan debt as "starting a race, and then the guy with the starter pistol uses the gun to shoot you in the leg."* Equity is about acknowledging these large societal gaps exist and providing

---

* Hasan Minhaj, writer and creator; Richard A. Preuss, director. "Student Loans,"

pathways to overcoming them. Equity is about bridging the opportunity gap and ensuring we're not making decisions based on prestige or access. Instead, we're looking at talent and capability more holistically.

General Martin Dempsey, former chairman of the Joint Chiefs of Staff, wrote: "If people don't feel like they belong to your group, department, company, or corporation, they easily can and probably will find something else to believe in and belong to. The most important responsibility of leaders—no matter how busy they are and how many other priorities demand their attention—is to make their people feel like they belong."*

So, what is belonging and how do we build it? Researchers R. F. Baumeister and M. R. Leary define belonging as "the feeling of security and support when there is a sense of acceptance, inclusion, and identity for a member of a certain group or place, and as the basic fundamental drive to form and maintain lasting, positive, and significant relationships with others."† Today many of us are compensated not for our ability to move something from here to there, but for our ability to think, solve problems, and achieve results through others. If we look back at what we know about the brain, we can't possibly contribute our best ideas if we are in the primitive or even emotional parts of our brains. We need this sense of belonging to get to the High-Performance Zone, and we need to build relationships to remain there.

In this chapter, we're going to focus on belonging through two lenses. First, how do we as individuals insist on belonging through authenticity at work? Showing up as our authentic selves builds our sense of belonging and supports the conditions for others to do the same. Second, what are the symbols of connection and belonging that exist in the organization? My colleague Catherine Nelson, general manager of our Australia

---

Patriot Act, season 2, episode 3, aired February 24, 2019. Los Gatos, CA: Netflix Studios.

* Martin Dempsey and Ori Brafman. *Radical Inclusion: What the Post-9/11 World Should Have Taught Us About Leadership.* Missionday, 2018.

† R. F. Baumeister and M. R. Leary, "The Need to Belong: Desire for Interpersonal Attachments as a Fundamental Human Motivation." *Psychological Bulletin* 117, no. 3 (1995): 497–529. https://www.talentinnovation.org/publication.cfm?publication=1640.

office, says, "Leaders create culture through all of their actions and inactions, including what they say and don't say." As leaders, we must ask ourselves: How are we perpetuating belonging through language, policies, and procedures, and representation across the organization? We know people are unable to contribute their best if they do not feel a sense of belonging—if they feel as if they can't be their authentic selves for fear of not "fitting in" or that the odds are stacked against them as they look ahead at their careers. Proactively building a sense of belonging across the organization can support a shift to high performance.

Authenticity at Work

Author and activist Marianne Williamson said, "As we let our own light shine, we unconsciously give other people permission to do the same. As we're liberated from our own fear, our presence automatically liberates others." *

Early in my sister-in-law's career, she didn't wear her wedding ring to job interviews because she worried it would negatively affect her chances of landing the job. She had seen that negative impact for others, an employer selecting a candidate because they didn't have a family and could presumably be more likely to prioritize work. Because of these experiences, she didn't feel like she could be authentic at work.

Catalyst, a global nonprofit working with some of the world's leading companies to build workplaces that work for women, defines emotional tax as "the heightened experience of being different from peers at work because of your gender and/or race/ethnicity and the associated detrimental effects on health, well-being, and the ability to thrive at work." † We presume that this tax exists across all manner of identifiers

---

* Marianne Williamson, *A Return to Love: Reflections on the Principles of "A Course in Miracles."* San Francisco: HarperOne, 1996.

† Dnika J. Travis and Jennifer Thorpe-Moscon, *Day-to-Day Experiences of Emotional Tax Among Women and Men of Color in the Workplace*. Catalyst, February 15, 2018; https://www.catalyst.org/research/day-to-day-experiences-of-emotional -tax-among-women-and-men-of-color-in-the-workplace/.

and differentiators, from having a disability to being the only person without a college degree on a team.

This feeling of constantly having to be on guard disrupts sleep patterns, reduces the sense of psychological safety, and diminishes the ability to contribute to work. As an example, a Black participant in one of our *Unconscious Bias* work sessions discussed how he accommodates White people in his personal and professional life by making himself smaller, speaking softly, and not making sudden movements. As he shared his experience, my own heart rate went up. My husband, six-four and built like a linebacker, has shared a similar reality with me. He is hyperaware of his place in the world, down to the details of where he is placed in a room, the volume at which he is speaking, and any manner of movement. This kind of self-monitoring takes an enormous toll.

While it is incumbent on employers to create conditions in which we can be authentic, there is also a growing movement and trend toward pushing for authenticity at work on an individual level. This movement at the employee level has influenced how organizations prioritize authenticity in order to remain competitive in recruitment and retention of top talent. The effort of hiding parts of yourself makes it impossible to be open and vulnerable—a requirement for connection—and individuals practicing authenticity can shift the conditions in a workplace just as profoundly as the actions of a leadership team.

My professional experience, particularly in my formative years, was quite different from my sister-in-law's. In college, I had an incredible boss named Martine who took it upon herself to show me what authenticity at work looked like. I worked in the Student Activities Center (now called the Office of Student Life) at George Washington University. I was responsible for supporting student programs focused on inclusion, and worked with my boss to launch a series called REAL Conversations, covering topics from race to socioeconomics. Martine and I met weekly to review my tasks, but early on, she introduced a more substantive quarterly conversation. She made a worksheet and asked that I consider my goals, not just in my role as a student activities coordinator, but also in other facets of my life: financial, family, academic, travel, and work. Each quarter we met not just to review my goals, but also hers. She shared her struggles and successes, and coached me through some of my own. This simple dialogue didn't take a lot of time, but it had a huge impact on me. Martine showed me that there was a place for my whole self at work and that all of my goals were intrinsically tied together. She knew that I couldn't possibly be in the High-Performance Zone if my cell phone got cut off (again!) or if I was worried about a class I was struggling in. She gave me permission to be authentic.

Although I haven't been in a job interview for years, historically I have been unapologetic about my family and most other things about myself. This was not the case for Mark as a Boomer or Anne as a Gen Xer. There's been a sea change at work concerning our comfortableness with authenticity; in fact the cultural norm now is "bring your whole self to work." There is no longer a firm boundary between work and life. I intentionally talk about my kids as part of my story. My oldest motivated me to get my MBA. My youngest has helped me with my work-life balance (because a toddler doesn't care if you're tired when you come back from a business trip!). I talk about my children as strengths. They inspire me and help me do and be better, and I want anyone I work for to know that we're a full package. They are such a big part of who I strive to be. Imagine how limiting it would be if I didn't feel like I could speak about them.

In the entertainment industry, Grammy Award–winning artist Janelle Monáe shines as an example of authenticity. When the world first met her, she wore a "uniform" of black and white. "A lot of it had to do with me wanting to have a uniform like the working class, like my mom and my grandmother," Monáe told *The Huffington Post*.* In this case, Monáe brought the context of her family into her professional presence, connecting her current reality as a global music star to her identity and background.

Being your authentic self at work is the first step to belonging. It is the open part where you are transparent and honest about your identity: who you are, what fuels you, and how you communicate. It means you let your colleagues in; they know your partner's name, your love

---

* Julee Wilson, "Janelle Monáe Honored at Essence Dinner Party, Explains Signature Black-And-White Style." *Huffington Post,* April 5, 2013; https://www.huffpost .com/entry/janelle-monae-essence-dinner-party_n_3021450.

of ski vacations, and your excitement about that new car. They know you're worried about your grandma and have strong feelings about X, Y, or Z. And they know how you're feeling about the work you're doing and which ideas and projects you're most excited about. The opposite of authenticity is an environment where you have to apologize for your existence. Apologizing for your body, your identifiers, your background, or your personality is inherently limiting, if not damaging. Does this mean we no longer have boundaries between our work and personal lives? Certainly not. The movement in favor of authenticity is a departure from traditional workplace norms around the separation of work and personal life, but it doesn't mean everything about your life is public. Instead, it means you don't feel the need to hide important components of your life or perspectives you may have that would be helpful to share at work. We shouldn't have to make choices between our authenticity and our contribution to the workplace.

Indicators of Belonging

Organizations and leaders are responsible for setting the conditions for belonging. The idea of belonging can feel like a vague or an abstract concept, so how do we as leaders *act* on it? You can assess a few elements of the workplace as symptoms of healthy or unhealthy levels of belonging. Use them as starting points for progress.

Language

Recently I was delivering our *Unconscious Bias* work session to a client, and we were discussing issues relevant to the LGBTQ+ community. A participant raised his hand and said, "What the heck is PIA?" He'd seen the acronym LGBTQPIA in another context. I explained that it stood for "pansexual, intersex, and asexual." He expressed frustration that he had to learn and use so many new, seemingly ever-changing terms. I replied, "I understand it can feel you're having to learn a new alphabet sometimes, but think of it this way. My name is Pamela, and it's important to me. It's more than just a label—it's part of my identity and who I am. Taking the time to learn my name feels respectful to me, a basic courtesy, and I will do my best to reciprocate."

As our conversation continued, it was clear his concern was not remembering the words but whether this was another step in "politically correct" language and how he'd even know which word to use to describe someone. When we think about "politically correct" terms, I've found it helpful to get out of our own head about it. Identity is as personal to us as our name, so just as you would call everyone by the name they asked to be referred to by, you should also employ the identifiers they ask you to use as well. If you're unsure which pronoun or identifier to use, follow the other person's lead. When in doubt, using their name will never fail you.

As is true in the areas of sexual orientation and gender identity, the words we used to describe intellectual and developmental disabilities have changed. In 2009, two youth leaders started a campaign called Spread the Word to End the Word, which according to their website focused on "addressing a particularly powerful form of exclusion: the word 'retard(ed).' Over ten years, leaders and self-advocates collected millions of digital and physical pledges to end the R-word. Each was a personal commitment to acknowledge the hurt caused by the R-word and to be respectful in the words and actions taken towards people with intellectual and developmental disabilities. With leadership from Special Olympics and Best Buddies International, and support from hundreds of other advocacy organizations, the campaign grew from a handful of events in 2009 to reach thousands of schools by 2018 and is now called Spread the Word: Inclusion."[*]

These are examples of terms that are evolving. With a little bit of interest and a quick internet search, we can learn the term that is preferred, most current, or appropriate. But the reality is that most groups aren't monoliths, and there are cases where a "correct" term doesn't exist. Racial and ethnic groups can be referred to in various ways—for example, First Nations, Indigenous, or Native American; Hispanic, Latino, or Chicano; or Black or African American (and this is nowhere near an exhaustive list). When in doubt, listen for a cue from the person

---

[*] About Spread the Word (February 25, 2020). Retrieved from https://www
.spreadtheword.global/about.

you're speaking with, or if appropriate, ask for their preference. Remember, a person's identifying term is a matter of personal preference and shouldn't be generalized. A friend of mine said, "I had a co-worker ask sincerely if they should say African American or Black, because they heard me say both. I explained we are all different, and with me, they could use the term Black. Fast-forward a month or so later, they were excited to share that they'd told another White colleague, 'We can say Black!' I had to reiterate that he could use it with me, but we are all different."

The impact of language in formal workplace policies is obvious. The difference between terms such as "maternity or paternity leave" and "parental or bonding leave" is significant. The language opens up the boundaries of this benefit to include the many circumstances in which a person might welcome a child. These best practices really come down to "people first" language—language that puts the person first broadens versus language that narrows. For example, we can choose words that include more people, such as "team" instead of "ladies and gentlemen."

MARK

Recently I ordered an Uber to get to the airport. The app confirmed my pickup with the make and model of car, the car's license plate number, and the driver's name. I always confirm the driver's name when I get in the car for safety reasons.

This time, the name was very unusual. I practiced it a few times before the driver arrived to make sure I pronounced it correctly. When I got in the car, I asked, "Ogoguantua?" He said, "Yes, are you Mark?" I said yes, and we went on our way.

After a couple of blocks, he said, "Can you say my name again?" At his request, I repeated it. Then he said, "Thank you. I moved here from Africa a little over a year ago. I've been driving for Uber for six months, and you're the first rider who has actually said my name."

Names can be a very powerful thing. It's probably the one word that people most want to hear, and when we take the time to get it right, we can implicitly communicate to others that they belong.

ANNE

I worked for a leader back in the 1990s who would always reference his organization as "the women and men on our team," and he consistently opened meetings large or small with "ladies and gentlemen." He had a military background, and I always respected the grace in which he approached his role. So of course I started to emulate him. I felt that using these words helped personalize leadership in an elegant way.

Fast-forward to today. I recently read an assertion that 25 percent of Generation Z (born 1995–2019) will shift their gender identity at least once in their life.* I realized the language that had once resonated with me in the nineties was inadvertently exclusionary today. Consciously, I've now altered my own language accordingly to ensure that I demonstrate my commitment to all people. I now say, "Ladies and gentlemen and all people," as well as "her or him or they," and I'm mindful of consistently adding the phrase "all team members" explicitly in my conversations, town halls, and speeches when referring to groups—whether they're my own or otherwise.

Words matter. And what's appropriate and inclusive evolves and changes over time. It's essential to listen, watch, learn, engage, and reengage.

Policies and Procedures

An organization's policies and procedures have real and disparate impact on the people in the organization. Diversity management consultants Mark Kaplan and Mason Donovan share a story about a client who was trying to reduce travel expenses, with unintended consequences:

> One easy target was premium parking at airports. A policy was put in place requiring all employees to use the economy lot. . . .
> Instead of seeing a decrease in travel expenses, the company started to see it creep up for some employees while for others

---

* Sylvia Ann Hewlett, Ripa Rashid, and Laura Sherbin, *Disrupt Bias, Drive Value: A New Path Toward Diverse, Engaged, and Fulfilled Talent*. Los Angeles: Rare Bird Books, 2017.

it dropped off altogether. During one of our sessions with the client, the topic came up, and we quickly discovered that female employees were spending an extra day on travel so they could return in the morning instead of the dark of night. They did not want to trek out to an isolated parking area at a late hour. In addition, [employees with disabilities] found managing the buses and massive parking lots a huge physical challenge, prompting them to forgo travel that may have moved the company forward. An inclusive lens was soon added to all travel policy decisions. For this particular policy, the company simply added the line, "We trust employees will make the best decision with regard to this policy when it comes to their safety or physical limitations."* [Note: To be even more inclusive, this organization could use the term "physical abilities," rather than "physical limitations."]

Similarly, a few months ago, I was working with a hospital system in Upstate New York exploring this idea of inclusive policies. We talked about a mandatory online training on safety that was required annually. There are employees in the hospital who don't need to be proficient in reading English to do their jobs but do need to complete this training. So every year, there was a group of personnel who were asked if they could read English, because they hadn't completed their mandatory training. They were then brought into a live session to complete their requirement, where the e-learning was projected onto a screen and painfully read aloud, a dreaded and awkward experience for all involved. One of the organization's Learning Management System (LMS) administrators creatively addressed this situation, deciding to add voice-over capability to the training as well as voice-over in multiple languages. This wasn't particularly onerous for him, fell within the scope of his role, and made a huge impact for traditionally invisible groups at the hospital. This practice has also broadened the type of learning this audience now has access to, as the LMS team has onboarded it more broadly across their training catalog.

---

* Mark Kaplan and Mason Donovan, *The Inclusion Dividend: Why Investing in Diversity and Inclusion Pays Off,* 2nd ed. Salisbury, NH: DG Press, 2019, 89.

To increase the inclusiveness of your policies and procedures, circulate drafts to team members of various identifiers and life circumstances and ask for their feedback. A caveat, though: Getting honest feedback requires a culture of trust, one in which people feel it's safe to tell the truth. Have you created that environment? When people have raised concerns about policies in the past, have leaders listened to that feedback, assessed it carefully, and acted on it?

Representation

Representation matters. As Pulitzer Prize–winning author Junot Díaz said, "If you want to make a human being into a monster, deny them, at the cultural level, any reflection of themselves."*

I sometimes work with organizations who tell me, "We have a very inclusive yet homogenous culture. You won't see the diversity, but we are inclusive in all of our practices, and this is a great place to work." I would push against that a bit. If the organization is not diverse, can it truly be inclusive? A sense of belonging is key to our overall sense of wellness as human beings. When people find themselves in the "only" category—when they don't see themselves reflected in the organization, in its customers, or in its leadership—this absence can impact how they define their possibilities. Many people have stories and examples to this effect. Working for someone like themselves helped them see and believe in their own possibilities. Representation demonstrates that an organization is upholding at least the infrastructure of connection— and that includes seeing yourself reflected across the organization and across its clients in a meaningful way. It includes customers seeing themselves reflected in your marketing and advertisements and points of contact they work with. In the public sector, it includes constituents seeing themselves represented in the policies and decisions made by their elected officials and other public servants. It includes not just who is in the organization, but who is making decisions in the organization.

---

* Junot Díaz, speech presented at Bergen Community College, Paramus, New Jersey, October 19, 2009; https://www.nj.com/ledgerlive/2009/10/junot_diazs_new _jersey.html.

A colleague of mine was facilitating our *Unconscious Bias* work session at the headquarters of a major corporation that sold apparel. As part of her preparation, she went on the organization's website and saw a rainbow flag and rainbow gear with the corporation's logo. She then called her local store and asked if they had these items in stock. The associate was adamant that they didn't sell this line and didn't even know it existed! It is in situations like this where authenticity comes up to the organizational level. Most firms have diverse public-relations campaigns and a beautiful website with all the right stock images containing the perfect balance of people, but does this representation run throughout the organization? Is it real? If it isn't, as a leader, consider what you can do to intentionally influence or change that.

ANNE

You may have heard the phrase "You cannot be what you cannot see." Do you believe this? If we see more people like us who are in roles, positions, and organizations around us, it stands to reason that we will have an increased sense of belonging. Why? Because we feel "connected" to them because of some common ground. This isn't simply a gender, ethnic, or a generational statement. Think about it. Don't you have some automatic affinity to others who have the same alma mater as you? Don't you have some inherent bond with others who majored in the same thing at college? How about if you're from the same town? See what I mean? We as humans long for connection; we're built to seek the familiar and find some basis for relationships and growth with others. And when we have some similarity, we automatically feel more connected.

I recently had an opportunity to feature a *New York Times* bestselling author at my leadership kickoff. In our greenroom time together prior to her keynote and our fireside chat, we discovered that we were both Chinese American Jersey girls, Ivy League graduates, mothers of two daughters, and Asians married to non-Asians. Each of us had a sibling who was a doctor. Though we had started out as complete strangers, our authentic connection was evident, and it positively influenced our fireside chat.

After we spoke, I had numerous women of color in my organization tell me how empowering it was for them to watch us onstage together. Feedback from the entire audience was positive, but these women were particularly inspired. Representation matters. Connection is everything.

Chapter 5: Focus on Belonging
Reflection for Individuals

We can better make progress toward belonging by being aware of our starting point.

Think about your ability to be authentic at work and your own sense of belonging, then answer the questions below with a yes or a no.

	Yes	No
1. It's Monday morning and your colleagues are talking about their weekends. You feel completely comfortable sharing yours.		
2. When you have an idea to share, you're confident it will be taken seriously.		
3. When you disagree with someone at work, you're comfortable sharing your opinion.		
4. You look forward to going to work.		
5. You work with people you trust.		
6. When you think about your future in this organization, you see your goals are possible.		
7. If your colleagues and friends met, you think they'd get along.		
8. The organization treats people fairly.		

	Yes	No
9. You're connected to colleagues via social media.		
10. You have pictures of family and/or friends on your desk.		

Take note of your No answers. Some situations might be no because they don't apply to your circumstances—for example, you work out of a home office, so having pictures on your desk is less relevant. Or you don't have a social media presence, so you're not connected with colleagues digitally. For each No that applies, there is some friction—a point of tension that stops you from being your full authentic self and inhibits your sense of belonging. Consider what that friction or tension might be.

....

....

....

....

....

As you move through the rest of this book, think about what skills and tools you might use to change each no to a yes, particularly Chapter 11: "Courage to Cope." Ultimately, a sense of belonging is a critical component for high performance, and if that is compromised, we owe it to ourselves to find or build a workplace where we can make a shift.

Chapter 5: Focus on Belonging
Application for Leaders

If you directly ask a team member if they feel like they belong, you might not get candid feedback. As you help team members, focus on the signs of belonging covered in this chapter.

1. As you prepare for your next team meeting, find a few tangible examples of language, policies and procedures, and representation in your team and organization that include or exclude elements of belonging.

Language:

....

....

....

Policies and Procedures:

....

....

....

Representation:

....

....

....

2. In the meeting, explain what each concept means, then share a specific example of how that element shows up in your team or organization. Have your team discuss:

    • How inclusive is our team in terms of this element?

    • What are we doing well?

    • Where could we improve?

    Take notes below to prepare for the meeting.

....

....

....

3. As you conclude the meeting, you might share the results of your own belonging assessment from Chapter 5, "Reflection for Individuals." Give your team the opportunity to complete this same reflection and offer to discuss their results in your next round of 1-on-1s.

....

....

....

....

....

....

....

....

....

....

Chapter 6: Deploy Curiosity and Empathy

Research suggests that empathy is both an instinct as well as a learned skill that can be developed through coaching and practice. In fact, studies indicate that people experience varying degrees of empathy based on their backgrounds, and that empathy can be learned and enhanced at any age.

—Dr. Laura Belsten, internationally known expert and author of the Social + Emotional Intelligence Profile®

Recently I was interviewing two candidates for an open position. I walked down to the lobby to meet the first candidate, who was tucked into a corner, speaking softly into her phone. I smiled as I overheard the conversation, something about math homework that sounded a lot like the conversations I had with my own fourth grader. As I approached, I made eye contact and smiled warmly. The candidate quickly got off the phone and apologized while fumbling to put it away in her purse. I assured her, "I've been there. Haven't we all?"

We made our way to the elevator and chatted about the lives of busy working mothers. We discovered that we grew up not far from each other. As the interview started, the candidate stuttered through the first question, and I gave her an opportunity to answer again. "Interviews can be nerve-racking," I said, reassuring her that her credentials were excellent and there was nothing to worry about. I continued to encourage her through the interview. The candidate recovered and finished the rest of the interview strong. At the end of the interview, I felt great about the connection and thought she would be a great fit for our team. I really enjoyed the conversation. I liked her.

An hour later, I went down to meet the next candidate in the lobby.

This was my last meeting of the day, and by then, I was tired and keen to get the new position filled. I'd looked up this candidate on LinkedIn and saw his elite connections. As we shook hands, I immediately noticed his fancy watch. "Too fancy for someone at his level," I thought. "He must not have had to work for much in his life." We went up the elevator in near silence, politely smiling at each other along the way. I didn't have any strong connection with this second candidate.

As the interview began, I asked the same questions. Like the first candidate, he stumbled slightly with his answer. I thought, "He isn't prepared. He should have a better answer than that. He knew he was being interviewed today, and this is a pretty standard question." As we went through the questions, I compared his answers to those of the previous candidate. The interview lasted only thirty minutes, compared to this morning's seventy-five. At the end of the interview, I didn't have a good feeling. He just wouldn't be a good fit for our team.

Which candidate was the most qualified for the position? There's no way to tell based on this story. I said very little about the candidates' qualifications, capabilities, or experience. I did say quite a bit about how each candidate made me feel and whether they would "fit" on my team.

The word "fit" is something of a four-letter word when it comes to bias. Often leaders will say, "I can teach someone how to do the job, but I can't teach them to work within our culture." We don't mean to discredit the idea completely, but the big, broad bucket of "fit," if we aren't careful, is often more about *likability* than about *competence*.

Researchers at Stanford and Yale conducted a study around this very point, asking people to think of an important project they needed to work on and then to rank a group of hypothetical candidates in the order they'd select them to join the project. They distinguished candidates based on competence and likability.[*]

---

[*] Susan T. Fiske et al., "A Model of (Often Mixed) Stereotype Content: Competence and Warmth Respectively Follow from Perceived Status and Competition." *Journal of Personality and Social Psychology* 82, no. 6 (2002): 878–902; https://doi.org/10.1037/0022-3514.82.6.878.

People *said* they would pick competent people over likable ones. But what they *did* was quite different. Their first preference was highly competent, highly likable people, as expected. But their second choice was someone likable . . . but incompetent! And they were more likely to do the project alone than to choose to work with anyone unlikable, whether that person was competent or not.

The biggest challenge with this, as with my story, is that likability is not determined by facts, but by how we feel about a person, which in turn is often based on how similar they are to us (affinity bias).

The Skills of Curiosity and Empathy

As we meet people and enter new situations, our brains are sorting, mostly based on gut reactions. This sort is largely superficial and drawn from initial instincts, but the ramifications of that initial categorization can be vast.

Employing the skills of empathy and curiosity can help us check our assumptions and explore our thinking. It can also uncover biases we might have, as each connection point becomes fertile ground for increasing likability and moving us all to the High-Performance Zone.

Empathy is an interpersonal approach, putting yourself in other people's shoes. **Curiosity** is an intellectual approach to cultivating connection; it involves asking insightful questions, truly listening for responses, and building a conversation from those responses and commonality.

MARK

High empathy alone is too much about the other person. High curiosity alone is too much about me. Connectedness comes with the balance of both.

In the interview story, I had empathy with the first candidate. I saw a part of my own life reflected in her, and because of that connection, I was naturally curious, asking her questions, making eye contact, and listening intently to her responses. With the second candidate, I did not initially feel empathy, and consequently did not exhibit curiosity. Had I done so, I probably would have found a connection point. Maybe we both enjoyed running obstacle races, had children of similar age, or just really loved late-night TV. In a work context, perhaps we both had a similar view on collaboration or could cover gaps in each other's strengths. Perhaps I would have been more strategic and he more relationship-oriented, and in working together, we would have made clients feel cared for while achieving their organizational results. Because I did not deploy curiosity, I'll never know.

ANNE

One of the things I learned to do early in my career was to study my frustrations. Does that sound odd? Think about it: when you're frustrated, oftentimes you're frustrated by a person in a given situation. Take a moment to think about why. During times like these, I've been able to bring to the surface some of my own unconscious biases, which I've then been able to purposefully address to create a better outcome.

Here's an example. Several jobs ago, the team who reported directly to me was largely made up of people about the same age, except for one. This one team member was nearly two decades my senior. The rhythm of our group had us communicating primarily on email and sometimes text. However, this one individual would call me. His desire was to talk things through. At first, I found it annoying and less efficient. However, it wasn't long before I realized there was a lesson here for me. I had to overcome my bias that the way the broader group approached communication was the best way. Rather, taking the time to talk things through enabled us to establish and solidify our connection, and because I adjusted to his desired approach, we were able to build a strong foundational relationship that allowed our group to make incredible progress. From that point on in my career, I incorporated the grace of his approach into mine, and I've found that it has helped me to be a better leader.

Strategies for Empathy and Curiosity

Put Yourself in Others' Shoes

It's very easy to criticize other people without knowing the full picture. For example, a leader at FranklinCovey, "Sonya," had an employee suddenly showing up late to work after years of punctuality. Sonya was about to reprimand the employee, when she decided to dig deeper and find out what was going on. During a 1-on-1, Sonya learned that the employee's spouse had recently been diagnosed with diabetes and was struggling with insulin shots each morning, and he had to choose between getting to work on time and helping his wife. Sonya and her team member discussed ways they could add flexibility to his work schedule. By taking a little extra time to hear the whole story, Sonya was better able to address the performance problem and enhance her employee's well-being.

A former colleague of mine shared an example of how his leader demonstrated a remarkable lack of perspective and an inability to see the world from another's point of view. "When I was in my late fifties, I was invited to join a new department at work—I felt like it was a real compliment that I had the skills and talents this team wanted. My new boss was great, but early on he started asking me, 'So how much longer are you going to work?' This went on for some time, and he would often ask the question in front of others. Finally, in a private conversation after he posed the question once more, I replied, 'Do you *want* me to leave? You keep asking me that question.' That stopped the inquiries for a while, at least until our sales suddenly dropped and business slowed significantly. He asked me again how long I intended to keep working. I assumed it had to be because he was tasked with considering salaries and a possible reduction in head count. Maybe it was and maybe it wasn't because of head count, but it made me feel uncomfortable and nervous. I began to worry and question my own abilities. Does he think I'm not capable? Am I easy pickings to let go because I don't have decades still to work in the company? Can he hire someone younger and pay them less? Does that hurt my credibility? Does he consider me 'old school,' with one foot out the door? And how can he *not* understand how it feels being on the receiving end of that question—what if it was *his* boss doing the asking?"

Get to Know Other People's Stories

Is there someone you're currently struggling with personally or professionally? And do you know the whole story? Consider ways you can connect with that person and learn more about their perspective on the situation. You might be surprised by what you learn.

Keep Exploring

Moving out of our comfort zone allows us to grow and learn, and there are many ways to do this—from the type of media we consume to the sorts of conversations we have. The underlying question to ask yourself as you explore is "Does this challenge my paradigm?" AllSides.com works to "expose people to information and ideas from all sides of the political spectrum so they can better understand the world—and each other." A quick visit to their site will provide you with the day's headlines from a liberal, centrist, and conservative perspective—same headline, different lens and therefore words.

I consume a lot of media. The depth and breadth of stories on television and in movies, books, and podcasts are constantly pushing how I think about the world and people's experience. Get curious about learning more from the many resources available. This could include going beyond the curated list Netflix and Hulu give you, committing to read books by authors from different countries or backgrounds than your own, and searching for podcasts that give you a glimpse of what life is like for other communities. Other possible corners of your life to explore range from engaging in dialogue with your neighbor to joining a local civic or fraternal organization. Consider where you might have new conversations that push exploration.

MARK

In the early 1980s, I worked for Bank of Boston in Buenos Aires, Argentina, doing feasibility studies on proposed ATMs at branch offices throughout the country. I quickly fell in love with the country and its people.

It was a time of civil unrest, with hyperinflation at almost 1,000 percent per annum. Anyone paid in pesos with a bank account would lose almost half the value of their paycheck by the time it could be deposited. A loaf of bread cost 10,000 pesos or more. Eventually, the government attempted to stem the tide by cutting zeros off the currency, finally taking the more extreme measure of switching to a new currency altogether called the austral.

Before changing the currency and in an attempt to create national stability, President Leopoldo Galtieri played one of the last cards available to him and invaded the Falkland Islands, a string of islands off the coast of Patagonia whose sovereignty had been in dispute with the United Kingdom for a century. The war lasted just 74 days and cost Argentina more than 600 casualties before Argentina surrendered.

It was a fascinating time to live in Argentina and see the effects of bias on a personal and national level. The United States had sided with Margaret Thatcher and the Brits in the war. I was an American living there in a time when Americans weren't very well thought of. I worked hard to put myself in their shoes, attempting to understand their stories and use the skills of empathy and curiosity to keep exploring. I invested time and energy in embracing the culture, from the local attire to customs around which I organized my day. Of course, it was clear I was an American. And as a result, I suffered some backlash from the local population.

In their view, I was on the wrong side. I can't count the number of times I was screamed at, had things thrown at me, was spat upon, wasn't allowed to board public transit, and so forth. American schools and the homes of some Americans were even being bombed. A neighbor's house was targeted; luckily no one was hurt. It was the first time in my life that I'd been on the receiving end of bias, in this case conscious in a public way.

I learned it takes a lot of energy to constantly be vigilant about where you are, how you present yourself, and what you say. The emotional tax was significant: it's difficult to trust others and even yourself when you're on the receiving end of bias; it's hard to be your best self when so much of your energy is being devoted to self-preservation.

I've also since learned that bias doesn't have to be life-threatening to elicit all the same feelings of insecurity and inadequacy. This experience was transformational in my life and really awakened a deeper sense of empathy and curiosity. As a result of this experience, I often ask myself, "Who in my environment is feeling like an outsider, like they're on the wrong side or don't belong? How can I support their sense of belonging to bridge that gap?"

Chapter 6: Deploy Curiosity and Empathy
Reflection for Individuals

Curiosity

1. Identify a colleague, stakeholder, or customer you don't know well. You're professional and cordial to them but don't understand what motivates them or their decision making. Write down what you do know about them. What comes to mind when you think of working with them? How collaborative are they, what is their working style, what might they be good at, what do they seem to enjoy, and where might they struggle?

....

....

....

Empathy

2. When you're next with this person in a meeting or on a call, dedicate the first fifteen minutes of the conversation to getting to know them a bit better. Don't open with the most intense question; progress to it. Start safe and then dive deeper.

....

....

....

3. Ensure that you're demonstrating empathy: position yourself on equal footing, focus completely on the conversation (no phones or email!), and withhold judgment. Demonstrate curiosity by asking insightful questions, building on the words and feelings the other person shares, and connecting with your own thoughts and feelings.

....

....

....

4. If they ask you questions in return, be open and honest. Ensure that this conversation is of mutual benefit instead of having the person feel like they're being interrogated.

....

....

....

Getting to Know Other People's Stories

Remember that using empathy and curiosity to build connection is a process. It will take more than one conversation, and requires reflection and care on your part to continue to the process of nurturing curiosity and empathy.

5. After your conversation, complete the following:

    • What biases, assumptions, or preferences surfaced in this dialogue, both positive and negative?

....

....

    • What did you get right on the list above, and what did you get wrong?

....

....

Chapter 6: Deploy Curiosity and Empathy
Application for Leaders

One organization began every meeting with a communication minute. They were a technical organization, and their employee-engagement surveys were telling them that people felt like the organization struggled with communication, particularly at the leadership level. The leader spent the first bit of every meeting—whether it was a 1-on-1 or a thousand-person town hall—reinforcing one of their communication values and a personal insight as to why that value mattered to them. Or they would share how that value affected their recent interactions.

As a leader, consider how you could implement a connection minute.

1. Dedicate the first few minutes of every meeting to connecting with people. Ask a brief question that invites empathy, curiosity, and dialogue.

....

2. At the start of a new month or quarter, ask your team to share what they're most proud of and why. Ask them to brainstorm what their goals are for the period ahead. If the team has similar goals, consider creating a scoreboard to track those goals, support one another, and celebrate wins.

....

3. Share a personal anecdote in which you've learned something, and ask the team to contribute any similar experiences.

....

4. Share a recent interaction with customers or stakeholders that was personally meaningful and ask your team to do the same.

....

Chapter 7: Tap Into the Power of Networks

We're not asking anyone else to apologize for their success. But we are saying, "Open up a window and unlock the door for others."

—Kathryn Finney, CEO of Genius Guild

In 2019, writer, producer, and actor Issa Rae won the Emerging Entrepreneur Award at the Women in Film Annual Gala. In her acceptance speech, she satirically said, "I'm closing all doors behind me, so if you didn't make it in, oops, your bad. Figure it out. 'Entrepreneur' means I did [this] by myself."[*]

Issa Rae was joking, but she was expressing an unspoken (or spoken!) belief common to a lot of successful people. We often hear comments like "No one ever gave me anything" and "I got where I am through hard work." But that's simply a fallacy. At some point, someone gave each of us an opportunity, hired us, or listened to our ideas. A colleague gave us feedback. A special teacher encouraged us.

My third-grade teacher told my parents my writing was far above grade level and I would be a writer someday. She gave me the confidence that I could do something extraordinary with my talent. Clearly I'm still living off the high of that accolade!

---

[*] Women in Film, Los Angeles. June 13, 2019. *Issa Rae Receives the Emerging Entrepreneur Award at the 2019 Women in Film Annual Gala* [video file]. Retrieved from https://www.youtube.com/watch?v=Db1dPZ5abn4.

Our lives and careers are filled with moments like these, where someone said or did something that at a minimum influenced us and at a maximum set us on a path. This is the power of networks and the power of connection.

Sometimes the power of networks is in seeing or not seeing yourself in them. Women of color make up only 3 percent of the C-suite across the Fortune 500, and research shows that not seeing yourself reflected in leadership can inhibit the sense you might have that it's possible to work toward leadership positions.

Sometimes the power of networks is in knowing what to do in certain circumstances. For first-generation professionals, moving through the socioeconomic and cultural context of corporate life—while lacking the benefit of professional family members, internship experience in their youth, or other exposure to the unspoken rules of work—results in fewer promotions and lower compensation. Negotiating a salary, working toward a promotion, and building influence and informal authority are not intuitive skills. They are things we learn how to do, often through networks. For example, on my first business trip with FranklinCovey, I didn't know I was expected to pay for my lodging and expenses and submit them for reimbursement. I hadn't yet received a paycheck from FranklinCovey, and I didn't actually have the money. Thankfully, a quick call to our office manager remedied my ignorance about business travel, and she called the hotel with the team's corporate card.

I benefited greatly from those who opened their networks to me. I met Julienne, for example, when I was a client of hers. On paper, we didn't have much in common. She was in her fifties, born and bred in the U.S. military, and working in the corporate world. I was a young Afro-Latina, a first-generation American, and working in the public sector. We were of different ages, races, backgrounds, and socioeconomic groups. But when I brought FranklinCovey in to do some consulting work, she said to me, "Pamela, you let me know if you ever need a job. You have this scrappiness to you that we're always looking for." Eventually, the timing was right, and Julienne helped me join FranklinCovey, where I've been privileged to work for nearly a decade with increasing responsibility and results. Julienne's action was counter to all the data that says leaders pick protégés of their same race. So much about me was different from her, and she still saw something in me. If we hadn't made a connection and built on our existing network, the trajectory of my career would have been totally different. And as our relationship grew, it was clear we had more in common than might have been apparent at first blush: both professional women in sales, mothers fiercely connected to our families, competitors, and now friends.

Networks give us an advantage in work and in life. They're a powerful tool in pushing against the systemic impacts of bias. Networks help us cope with being on the receiving end of bias, find a sense of belonging, and build our cultural competence so we can make decisions based on fact and not instinct or feeling.

The power of networks is accelerated when we intentionally seek out opportunities to build perspectives different from our own. To evaluate the power of your network, let's clarify the different network categories: for our purposes, we're going to consider mentorship, coaching, sponsorship, and confidants. Each of these network components serves a different purpose, and we deploy curiosity and empathy differently within each category.

Mentorship

Mentorship is focused on skill building. A mentor is usually a person from whom you have something to learn, whether it be a more seasoned professional in your line of work, an expert in another line of the business, or someone with a specific skill you'd like to develop, like social media or project management.

Coaching

Coaching is about learning the playbook: strategizing about your career and learning more intangible skills like developing executive presence, expanding influence, and building your brand. While mentorship is about a mentor imparting specific knowledge to the mentee, coaching puts more emphasis on the person who is being coached setting goals and seeking feedback as opposed to gaining technical skill.

Sponsorship

Sponsorship is different from mentorship and coaching in that you are rarely present when you are sponsored. Sponsorship comes from someone with formal authority and influence above your own. Being sponsored means you are recommended. My husband works at the U.S. State Department and often refers to the seventeenth floor, where all the bigwigs work. On the seventeenth floor, leaders often talk about opportunities, assignments, and high-profile projects. Sponsorship is when your name comes up in those meetings, when an executive ties your reputation to theirs. It's an endorsement.

Confidants

Plainly put, mentorship is about skill building, coaching is about strategy, and sponsorship is about reputation. We've added confidants to the list because—as it relates to inclusion, equity, and bias—making progress requires a safe space. A confidant is someone you trust implicitly and with whom you can share your thoughts around being on the receiving end of bias or having biases yourself.

Sometimes the confidant is a trusted colleague and sometimes a friend. Ideally, it's not one person, but a few people. For example, I was in a book club for many years comprised of college-educated professional women of color, mostly partnered and all with kids. The opportunity to confide in them about our unique position—most of us working in predominately White, male-dominated organizations, juggling partners, kids, ambition, and sleep—was invaluable during that time in my life and career. I also have a few female confidantes, colleagues at FranklinCovey, with whom I discuss our role as women in the organization and the unique nuances of our organizational culture. Because even the most effective and collaborative of workplaces has unspoken norms and expectations that must be navigated in order to progress, I've had the privilege of participating in several structured development programs for sales and high-potential leaders. Again, I have built a small network of confidants from these programs with whom I can discuss the details of our role.

MARK

Mentorship can do the work that an organizational culture might be lacking. I started my career in a very small, traditional organization where I felt strongly that my gayness could be held against me if I'd divulged it. It wasn't until I worked for a specific manager that I felt it was safe for me to share this part of my identity. He showed real interest in getting to know me, developing me, and supporting my career. He was vulnerable himself, which affirmed that I could also be vulnerable; a real mentor, at times a confidant. There's impact in a leader's ability to model and build a sense of belonging.

ANNE

The importance of these different roles can be highlighted as follows: Coaches *talk to* you. Mentors *talk with* you. Sponsors *talk about* you. You will have bosses, teammates, colleagues, and others who may or may not fall into these categories. Few will serve as true confidants—and you must be sure that those you view as confidants truly are. I've seen many people make that mistake, as I have too.

Think about the differences in these roles. Coaches work with you on a skill—they focus on helping you do something or work on something, and give you guidance and support. With coaches, you are focused on a skill, a relationship, an organizational dynamic, a situation, or something similar. Coaching could be in the moment or ongoing. Mentors talk with you; with mentors, you expose more of your whole self, and they are often trusted confidants. They can serve as a sounding board and give you insights, expand your perspective, and talk things through with you in a way others can't. Mentors can be situational or sustained. The most important thing about mentors and mentees is it's a two-way relationship based on connection and trust. You can't "cold-call" a mentor (you'd be surprised at the number of times this happens). What do I mean by this? A mentorship takes time to develop and requires some work and investment. And whether someone can or will be a mentor to you at the outset—without an understanding or basic appreciation for each other—cannot be answered as a simple yes or no like a telemarketing outreach. Another key insight

I've had about mentors is the fact that mentors can be found in all aspects of our life, not just inside the companies we work for.

Sponsors are perhaps the most elusive of roles for many. Sponsors are only earned. You can't randomly ask someone to be your sponsor. Sponsors can represent you "at the table" when promotions are being discussed, special projects come up, and key decisions are being made. Sponsors know your work firsthand. Sponsors put their name alongside yours and vouch for you because they know what you've done and what you're capable of. In my experience, sponsors are most commonly earned through your direct management chain and through cross-functional exposure and positioning.

Your networks—that is to say, your connections—are an integral part of who you are, and they play a key role in helping you realize your fullest potential.

Strategies for Expanding Your Network

An organization can build a great diversity recruiting program, but if people don't have an internal network that reflects that diversity, they won't stay. Without networks, you will not retain diverse employees, they will not perform at their best, and they will not get promoted through the ranks.

Some of my clients ask, "Is it bad if I have a very homogenous network?" It's not bad. It doesn't make you a bad person. But you might be missing out on the power in diversity. In my time at the Department of Defense, I heard a lot of national-security examples that highlighted this. With the Bay of Pigs, the decision makers around the table were all men of the same ethnicity and profession; they were even educated at the same one or two affluent schools in the northeastern United States. And history tells us they didn't make the best decisions. According to the 9/11 Commission Report, one of the biggest failings of the intelligence community leading up to the terrorist attack was a lack of diversity. We had built our intelligence community to address Russia or the Soviet bloc, which was a big entity with lots of influence. But Al-Qaeda was a small entity. It carried out guerrilla warfare, a different way of operating. We didn't even have native Arabic speakers who could understand the nuances of the language and culture. It's not that homogenous networks are bad; it's that there's so much value when we expand beyond that.

These are examples pertaining to national security; the stakes were clearly high. But even in informal environments, bias and specifically groupthink can seep in. In 1983, a group of sixteen retired women formed the Beardstown Business and Professional Women's Investment Club. The Beardstown Ladies went on to report annual returns of 23.4 percent since their inception, well above the S&P 500 Index during the same period, and published a series of books, beginning with the 1995 title *The Beardstown Ladies' Common-Sense Investment Guide: How We Beat the Stock Market—And How You Can Too*. Unfortunately, their success was soon debunked by a journalist. PricewaterhouseCoopers conducted an audit and found that the club had made a computer-formula error in calculating returns, and the returns, at just 9.1 percent, were actually well below the S&P 500 Index. While the club issued an apology and a disclaimer on all of its books, the publisher, Hyperion, was subject to a class action lawsuit that resulted in an exchange of all Beardstown Ladies books for other books by Hyperion.

At the end of this chapter, you'll find a tool to help evaluate your own network. When you complete that, push past the instinct to say your network is good as is. Consider opportunities to build more robust networks of mentorship, coaching, sponsorship, and confidants from up, down, and across your organization and your life.

Once you identify the opportunities, you can deploy these strategies to bridge the gaps.

Use the "Google Machine"

I had a friend in college who referred to the internet as the "Google Machine." When you have a question, the Google Machine always has an answer. Internet-based networks can be superficial in nature (who really has 3,000 friends?), but they can also be a bridge that connects you to people and places you might never encounter in your day-to-day life. For many years, I worked for a global nonprofit dedicated to supporting friendship, housing, and jobs for people with intellectual and development disabilities, Best Buddies International. Today my son has an intellectual disability. And yet, I don't have anyone in my personal or professional network from whom I can learn more. But I do have the Google Machine, where I can find organizations like Specialisterne, which reframes neurodiversity in terms of its abilities and focuses on the competitive advantage of individuals on the autism spectrum at work. I can also join discussion groups on Facebook run by adults on the autism spectrum, which pushes my thinking around autism, language, and communication.

Expand Clubs Beyond School

We often think of clubs, groups, and associations as something we do in high school or college, but it's never too late to join or form a club (or network, if you will). It could be a professional association, an employee resource group within your organization, or a networking organization. Consider how many hours a week you spend with other people. Is it always the same people? Clubs provide an opportunity to seek out more.

ANNE

Perhaps it's stating the obvious that nothing in this life is accomplished alone. As we think about our younger years, we had the support of others, typically adult figures—whether parents, family friends, teachers, community leaders, or others.

As young professionals, you find that the network of people around you evolves, and your boss and your direct teammates are most important. However, you should realize that there are many others who can have influence on you, whether directly or indirectly. Whether consciously or unconsciously, we often miss the indirect opportunity—not necessarily thinking about the network of our networks—as our careers evolve, our reputations and personal brands are built. I have coached and mentored numerous people over the course of my career who have not proactively and consciously thought through the why and why not of maximizing an opportunity, whether it's a promotion, a special project, appropriate credit for their work, or something else. Recognizing that you can't rely solely on one person on your team—many put too much emphasis on their boss—and realizing that your career is yours to manage can help you come up with a more purposeful approach to networking and the development of meaningful, impactful relationships. You need many different types of people to fulfill different roles along the way (and by the way, you owe it to others to do the same).

As a practical example, consider a situation where you are a member of the team working on a project. Your role is clear, and you know who your team members are. Perhaps it's also clear who the team leader is. However, as a team member, are you narrowly focused on your piece of the puzzle, or have you taken an opportunity to consider the framing of the project itself? What's the view of the customer? Who and what must provide input into your team for it to be successful? What does success look like, not just tactically for the team, but in terms of true business outcomes? Are the measurements clear? Are there biases in the system, or even biases being driven by team dynamics that represent an opportunity to reframe the approach for a better outcome? Thinking through these types of questions and others can help reframe an opportunity to broaden your network as well as your input by gaining other perspectives beyond the obvious ones.

Increase Your Inputs

As we mentioned earlier, confirmation bias occurs when we only recognize information that affirms our existing beliefs as opposed to new information that might challenge our perceptions. Public figures, academics, and thought leaders can serve as part of our network in a broader way. For example, I listen to a handful of podcasts that seriously influence my thinking around politics, work, and money. In a sense, I have a weekly conversation with the people who run these podcasts. Consider what you read, watch, and listen to; then broaden where you get information. If you increase the inputs, you'll naturally increase the output in terms of how you're connecting and building networks with others. As an aside, what you read, watch, and listen to can build bridges to mentors, sponsors, coaches, and confidants through discussion and dialogue. Let's call that a fringe benefit!

Ultimately, leveraging the power of networks as a tool for building connection and mitigating bias is about getting out of your comfort zone. You might be thinking, "I'm very busy. I've got a lot of things going on." But here's the good news: expanding your network can take as little as a few minutes. Who can you connect to next?

Chapter 7: Tap into the Power of Networks
Reflection for Individuals

1. Consider the network categories outlined in this chapter. List one or two people in each—mentor, coach, sponsor, confidant. Who holds that title for you? For whom do you hold that title?

	For me:	I am this to:
Mentor		
Coach		
Sponsor		
Confidant		

Do you have any gaps or blank spaces? Could you list two or more in all of these categories?

....

....

....

2. Now think about your identifiers. Count the people who are the same as or different from you in various dimensions (such as age, ethnicity, etc.).

....

....

....

3. What do you notice about who you choose to connect with or who chooses to connect with you? How does who you connect with impact or affect your influence?

....

....

....

4. What commitments will you make to fill in the gaps?

....

....

....

....

....

....

....

....

....

....

....

....

....

....

....

....

Chapter 7: Tap into the Power of Networks
Application for Leaders

As a leader, your network has impact on your individual influence, but it also has a larger impact on the organization, what leadership looks like, how included people feel on their teams, and whether people have a sense of belonging in and influence on the organization.

1. List ten people from your professional network you interact with: people above you, below you, across, at the same level, at client sites, or from other divisions. Challenge yourself—this is not an exercise in "Well, I work with this one Black person . . ." This is who you go to when you have a problem or a big challenge to solve. Who comes to you when they have a dilemma or when they need coaching or mentorship? Who are the go-to people in your network, and for whom are you the go-to person?

   1. ....

   2. ....

   3. ....

   4. ....

   5. ....

   6. ....

   7. ....

   8. ....

   9. ....

   10. ....

2. Count the people who are the *same as or different from you* in various categories. What do you notice about who you choose to connect

with or who chooses to connect with you? How does who you connect with impact or affect your influence?

....

....

With your identified list of people, count the number of people who are the same and different from you in each of the categories below.

Same	Different		Same	Different	
		Age Group			Physical Ability
		Color			Physical Appearance
		Education Level			Political Views
		Expertise			Race/Ethnicity
		Family Status			Religion
		Gender			Sexual Orientation/ Identity
		National Origin			Socioeconomic Status
		Personality			

What do you notice about who you choose to connect with?

....
....
....
....

How does who you connect with affect your influence?

....
....
....

Chapter 8: Navigate Difficult Conversations

You do not have the right to be a manager or leader of people if you do not summon the courage to discuss the undiscuss-ables. Nobody is born courageous. We're born cowardly, and it's with practice, mistakes, and role-playing that you become more adept at leading difficult conversations.*

—Scott Miller, bestselling coauthor of *Everyone Deserves a Great Manager*

Rarely are discussions around bias easy—but they can be productive, trust-building, and performance-enhancing, if we can conduct them from our thinking brains. But more commonly, difficult conversations about bias activate the primitive brain on both sides.

Those experiencing bias might be thinking, "The system is rigged against me. People like me don't have power, can't move up, don't lead projects, and don't make the big bucks." They feel that opportunity has been closed off, and because our professions are our main mechanisms for providing financially for ourselves, experiencing bias at work can threaten our ability to care for ourselves and potentially our families. Our primitive brains feel like our very survival is at stake.

Those who have not been subjected to bias can feel just as threatened: "None of that bias is my fault, as an individual. I'm not going to get

---

* Alissa Carpenter, "How to Embrace Your Mess as a Leader." Thrive Global, September 9, 2019; https://thriveglobal.com/stories/how-to-embrace-your-mess-as -a-leader/.

booted out because I don't look the right way. It feels like these conversations are about removing me." Again, a primitive, defensive mindset kicks in. No wonder these conversations can be so challenging!

What's amazing to me is these two sides see themselves as in opposition to each other, yet their experiences are quite similar. Both sides feel harm to their sense of belonging.

We can correlate the "temperature" of these conversations to our Performance Model. As our discussion gets more heated, both sides slip into the Limiting and Damaging Zones. In the Damaging Zone, we're completely closed off, defensive, and adversarial. Trust plummets to zero. Everyone's performance will inevitably suffer. In Limiting Zone conversations, people are tiptoeing around, misunderstanding intent, and getting frustrated; performance will still be inhibited, as trust is still low.

Our goal is to ensure that our discussions around bias move us to, or keep us in, the High-Performance Zone, where the intent of our conversations is understanding, empathy, and learning. We're clarifying assumptions and addressing misunderstandings. We might also be repairing the harm from previous limiting or damaging conversations around bias. We stay proactive, pausing between stimulus and response and choosing to act out of our thinking brain, not out of our emotional or primitive brains.

It can be done. Let's discuss how we can stay in the High-Performance

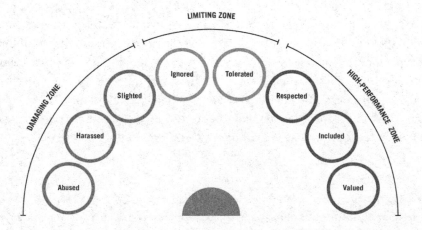

Zone, both when we need to bring up bias with a leader and when someone brings up bias to us. You may have formal policies and procedures to follow when conversations about bias arise, but on these pages, we're focusing on strategies that aren't merely compliance-based, but performance-enhancing.

When You Need to Bring Up Bias

If you're experiencing bias in the workplace, consider using these four strategies for navigating the conversation:

Ask Questions

If you sense a decision is being made from a place of bias, ask for more details, digging through impressions and feelings (where unconscious bias lurks) until you arrive at facts. For example, perhaps you think an older team member, Ed, is not being fairly considered for a promotion due to his age. Here's how you might navigate that conversation:

> **You:** Ed seems to be the most qualified candidate for the position. His record is strong, and he's eager to move up.
>
> **Hiring Manager:** I don't think he'd be the right fit for this position.
>
> **You:** What makes you think that?
>
> **Hiring Manager:** He doesn't seem like he could handle the job.
>
> **You:** Could you explain what you mean by "handle the job"?
>
> **Hiring Manager:** I don't think he'd be able to keep up with the travel requirements.
>
> **You:** Ed's current role requires 40 percent travel, and he's been hitting his benchmarks. To me that indicates he can handle the travel. Would you agree?

Easy to write as a hypothetical conversation—a little harder to do in real life! But the goal is to move from feelings, instincts, and impressions to more verifiable facts. You can use this strategy when you feel you're experiencing bias yourself as well. Perhaps *you* are the candidate who suspects you aren't being fully considered due to your age. Ask your manager, "Could you explain what I could do to secure the promotion in six months?" Keep probing until you reach some actionable steps.

ANNE

Have you heard of one of the top five things you should never ask a person of color? Some of you know exactly what I'm talking about.

"Where are you from?"

It's such an interesting question, isn't it? It comes up naturally in conversation when we are getting to know someone. Most often, when we ask it, we want to know where someone lives or where they grew up. These are all very logical and innocent things to inquire about. And that's how the majority of us would answer the question. However, in some cases, it's asked in a different context. Here's how this version goes:

Q: Where are you from?

A: I live in the DFW metro area, but I grew up in New Jersey.

Q: No, where are you *really* from?

A: Oh, you mean where I was born? I was born in the Midwest.

Q: No, where are you really, really from?

A: Oh, you mean my ethnicity. I'm Taiwanese Chinese.

Think about this interaction. The framing of it implies I'm from somewhere that is not here. To some, it may have a tone that you don't belong. I'll admit that in my early days, I was quite offended by this line of questioning. Young Anne was known to answer it in an abrupt way. Mature Anne realizes this is a teaching moment, which is why I end the series of questions above with:

A: And where are *you* really from?

Another version of this question that I and other people of color hear frequently is "What are you?" Think about that one. When you ask someone the question in that way, it again implies that you are not like me, so what are you?

Ninety-nine percent of the time, people aren't asking this question because they're racist. Rather, they don't know or understand the sensitivities. So don't assume the worst. Assume the best and educate. Have the conversation. You can bet that after the line of Q&A above, those individuals won't ask "Where are you from?" in the same way again.

Remember, our words matter. Intent matters. So if you're in the position of being the person who has asked these questions, think about how you can rephrase your inquiries in the future. Here are some better ways to be clear about what you're interested in:

"Where's home for you?"

"Where did you grow up?"

"What's your ethnicity?"

"Where did you go to school?"

"Where did your parents grow up?"

Note that I'm not suggesting that these types of questions are inappropriate, although some of them certainly would be in an interview. However, it's worth considering what's behind your inquiries. It's absolutely natural to want to get to know someone, especially as you're working to establish rapport. Just realize that some may not want to go down this path with you, and others may be sensitive to the approach. It's up to you to figure out how best to have that dialogue in the most constructive and positive way possible. By no means is it one size fits all, and it's important to be sensitive to the needs and reactions of others so that your approach in establishing connection is as effective as possible and aligned with whatever outcome you're striving for.

Tell Stories

Sometimes you need to discuss bias with someone who has an entrenched opinion about you or a situation. They can't even seem to hear you. Use the incredible power of narrative to build the empathy.

I once mentioned to a colleague that I was from the Dominican Republic, and she went on to talk about how terrible and impoverished it was when she'd visited thirty years ago. Of course I didn't think it was appropriate to describe the Dominican Republic as *terrible*. The Dominican Republic boasts the eighth largest economy in Latin America and the largest in the Caribbean. It is described by development experts as an upper middle-income developing country and has thriving mining, agriculture, trade, and tourism industries. So while the region of the country my colleague experienced had more poverty than she'd ever seen, her perception of the country was so limiting.

I could have challenged her perspective with the facts above and my own experiences across the country. Instead, I told my colleague about taking my son to visit my father in the Dominican Republic, how comfortable the trip was, the beautiful sights we saw that she never visited and didn't know existed, and was sure to include the modern amenities like the metro and the food scene in the colonial city. My story was more relatable than the data; I was countering my experience with hers. She was drawn in by the narrative of a daughter bringing her son to see his grandfather's home, and was able to emotionally understand how special that trip was. But if I just told her she was wrong about her own experience, I wasn't going to get anywhere.

Tear Down the Wall

MARK

I was born in 1960 and am solidly a Baby Boomer, a fact that has influenced my experience around identity. I remember watching the first humans set foot on the moon on our black-and-white TV in 1969, and getting my first pair of bell-bottom pants at the start of second grade. It was a time when bias against people of color, the LGBTQ+ community, women, and other marginalized groups was much more tolerated, and legal protections for these groups did not exist. My dad was an Air Force pilot who had served in Vietnam and my mother was a stay-at-home mom.

From a young age, I knew that I was different, and it wasn't until I was in my early teens that I realized what that difference was. I was gay, something that wasn't spoken of, much less represented in the mainstream media during those years. And at home, my only memories of my father's acknowledgment of gay people's existence was as the butt of his crass jokes. We always struggled to get along, and my strategy for dealing with this was to avoid conflict and him as much as I could.

I didn't come out to my parents until I was thirty-five, and as I'd expected, it didn't go well. There were no supportive words or statements of validation, only mandates of things I had to do to "fix my problem." After weeks of avoiding them both and really considering if I could disconnect from them completely, I decided to lean in to a very difficult conversation. I'd spent so much time inhibited by my father's very conscious bias and struggling with my own sense of worth, I just didn't want to feel like that anymore.

I reached out to my father and asked if we could talk in person, setting two conditions: first, we be completely honest with each other, and second, we don't attempt to "solve" anything, but just try to understand each other. We each prepared a list of questions with the caveat that we'd be completely honest in response. I told him, "If you don't want to hear the answer, don't ask the question!"

The next weekend he flew to Dallas and we spent the whole weekend together. We laughed, we cried, and we talked about things we had never dared talk about before. At the end of the weekend, he said to me, "I've always known there was a wall between us, but I never knew what it was. Now that I'm beginning to understand it, I look forward to finding ways to tear it down!"

While stepping into conflict is still not my natural inclination, I've since tried to apply that same language to conflict in my personal and professional life. I ask myself, "What's the wall between us?" Sometimes that wall is a bias, and asking the question allows us to surface bias that might not come up otherwise. Once we create a space to acknowledge bias, we can partner to tear down the wall, strengthening relationships and building connection in the process.

Bring In an Unofficial Mediator

You don't always have to put yourself in the fray. There's a time and a place to bring in someone senior for help, if you have a relationship of trust with that person. Let that trust work for you in this difficult conversation.

Years ago, I needed to raise a sensitive issue of bias with a leader several levels above me. I could have approached that person directly with the above strategies, but in this case, it was much more valuable for me to let a mutual associate, "Elena," have that conversation. Elena had high trust with that leader and me. I had a fully candid conversation with her; then she more effectively approached that leader about the issue herself. (This is a critical function of an ally, which we will cover in greater depth in Chapter 12.)

For Leaders: When a Team Member Brings Up Bias to You

Leaders are human. And in sensitive conversations, we're just as susceptible to the "fight, flight, or freeze" instinct as anyone else.

But as leaders, we are responsible for unleashing the performance of our team members, and reactive responses will plummet us down to the Limiting Zone. We must rise above our instinctual responses and effectively address bias when we see it in ourselves and when it's brought to our attention.

Listen, Listen, Listen

While addressing a class of midcareer Army graduates, four-star general Glenn Otis told the graduates he wanted them to remember only one thing during their upcoming military leadership. He pulled out an index card he carried with him at all times, which read, *When was the last time you allowed a subordinate to change your mind about something?* He then told the graduates, "I want you to remember this as you leave here today and rejoin the regular Army: be a good listener."*

Many leaders think they're good listeners, but in reality, they're just good at waiting for their turn to respond. We're not talking about that kind of surface-level listening here, but rather a high-level skill called Empathic Listening. It means listening with the intent to understand,

---

* Martin Dempsey and Ori Brafman, *Radical Inclusion*. Missionday, 2018.

not simply responding. Empathic Listening is a leadership competency, and it requires maturity, patience, and as General Otis emphasized, an openness to being influenced by your direct reports.

At FranklinCovey, chief people officer Todd Davis is our resident expert on this skill. In his bestselling book *Get Better: 15 Proven Practices to Build Effective Relationships at Work,* he writes: "While you're listening, you're not imposing your views on the person. You're not trying to figure out how to get them to see it your way. Instead, you're suspending your opinions long enough to really step into that individual's world and try to understand it from their point of view."*

When your team members are talking, don't outline your response in your head. Don't assess whether you agree or disagree. Focus solely on *understanding what they are saying and feeling.* Use simple phrases like "So you're saying . . ." Keep reflecting back what you hear until they agree that you thoroughly understand their point of view.

If you try to short-circuit this process and jump right to responding, you'll find emotions heating up quickly, trust eroding, and subsequent performance declining into the Limiting Zone. Empathic Listening takes extra time and effort, but as Stephen R. Covey said, "With people, fast is slow and slow is fast." The time pays off.

I believe that when we demonstrate understanding through Empathic Listening and reflective responses, both leader and team members are more likely to move into the thinking brain. Only then can we find solutions, build trust, and make progress on the bias at hand. Otherwise, expect the issue to metastasize.

ANNE

The reality is that you cannot empathize, learn, or grow if you're talking. Why? Because you're focused on yourself, not on who or what's around you. It's the old saying that we have two ears and only one mouth, so we should be listening at least two times as much as we're talking. It's

---

* Todd Davis, *Get Better: 15 Proven Practices to Build Effective Relationships at Work.* New York: Simon & Schuster, 2017.

true. Resist the urge to jump in. Listen fully and observe fully. Be in the moment. Then reflect—sometimes people just want a sounding board. They don't want your answer to the situation. While they may ask, "What would you do?" resist the temptation to take that question at face value. What they want really is your perspective so they can make the decision themselves. I always tell people who want a mentoring discussion with me that they should expect a lot of questions, as my role is to help and support them in figuring it out for themselves.

Allow for Emotions

Bias conversations can be emotional. But when someone raises an issue of bias, a leader's first instinct is often to tell them to calm down and/or tell the direct report that their message is getting lost in their emotion. Not only is that ineffective (when in human history has asking someone to calm down ever worked?), it's misguided. Emotion is germane to this type of conversation.

Empathic Listening includes understanding both the content and the emotion of the other person. When one of my children comes to me crying about a LEGO creation his brother has knocked down, I'll only prolong his upset by saying, "Calm down. You can rebuild it, and it wasn't that important." If I truly want him to move on to a solution, I need to acknowledge the validity of his emotion: "You worked hard on that, and I understand how upsetting it is that your brother didn't respect your stuff." We sometimes have the right intuition about parenting and forget to extend the same thoughtfulness to adults. As emotion rises over the course of the conversation, don't shut it down. Instead, reflect feelings and emotions back at the other person and let this emotion unfold to a solution.

Beware of Gaslighting

Gaslighting is a tactic used to make people question their version of reality. It can show up in difficult conversations if you feel defensive or disagree with the other person's version of events. For example, an employee might share that they feel like they are in the Limiting Zone because of their race or because they're the youngest member of the team. They might share examples of times their ideas were dismissed or insensitive jokes were made and the team laughed, or you as the leader laughed instead of pointing out that the joke was problematic. If you find yourself minimizing the thoughts and feelings of the other person, deflecting blame, declaring something didn't happen, or omitting details, you may be falling into this practice and accidentally gaslighting the other person. We're in particular danger of falling into gaslighting when we feel defensive or someone is questioning the motives behind our decisions or responses. Remember that when a team member brings up bias, your focus as the leader should be on their experience, understanding it, and partnering with them to make a shift to high performance. Gaslighting can feel like healthy debate from your perspective, but the person you're speaking with might feel you are minimizing their experience; this can push someone feeling in the Limiting Zone directly to the Damaging Zone. If you're finding it difficult to engage meaningfully with them, it may be time to step back and take a beat.

Take a Beat

You may need to separate yourself from the initial news before you respond—and there's nothing wrong with that. After you've listened empathically and the team member knows you understand their point of view, you do not have to address the issue that very moment. It's completely okay to say, "I need to take some time to think about this. Can we touch base on that again next week?"

Proactively Bring Issues of Bias to the Surface

The best leaders go beyond handling bias conversations well to proactively asking their team how bias might be affecting them and their performance.

A lot of leaders wonder how they do that. It's very simple—you have to ask. As writer Chimamanda Ngozi Adichie says, "If you don't understand, ask questions. If you're uncomfortable about asking questions, say you are uncomfortable about asking questions and then ask anyway."*

---

* Chimamanda Ngozi Adichie, *Americanah*. New York: Anchor Books, 2014, 406.

Note: Work with HR to clarify what you can and can't do within your workplace, then use the following strategies:

- **Ask only if you want the information.** If you seek feedback on bias then don't do anything about what they tell you, it's worse than not having asked for the information at all. Make sure you are mentally prepared for what you may hear.

- **Don't rely on an "open door" policy.** An open door is not a policy—it's just a door. It doesn't mean you're necessarily receptive to what happens when someone walks through it, or that you've created the time and space for them to actually talk with you.

    Most managers find that few team members take advantage of the offer—and it's not because there aren't any problems on the team. Given the power dynamics of the situation, you can't expect your direct reports to bring up difficult topics with the person responsible for their job security.

    Showing people you're interested has a much bigger impact than telling them you are. The best opportunity for these discussions is your weekly 1-on-1s, when you can ask thought-provoking questions and seek feedback. Use this time to watch body language and listen for what isn't said as much as for what is, then proactively initiate difficult conversations if you suspect something's off.

- **Rebalance power.** There is an inherent imbalance of power in 1-on-1s and other performance-management conversations. You can mitigate that by having the employee tell you what *you* can do better and what you're doing well: "I want to start here by saying my goal is to support you and to achieve results. I want to give you an opportunity to tell me one thing you'd like me to stop, start, or continue when it comes to how fairly and equitably our team runs." Asking them the question in advance of the conversation, perhaps via email or some other method, works even better. That allows them to gather their thoughts and more clearly articulate their points, as well as alleviating the feeling of being ambushed. If you say, "Tell me what's working and what's not," many people will tell you that everything is working and nothing is not working.

- **Be clear and transparent about what you do with the results, about what you can and cannot do.** For example, if a team member says, "The way raises are distributed is a problem," you might say, "Pay plans are above me; that comes from our CEO. I can advocate for that, but I can't personally change it." But if another team member reports, "I feel like the remote team members are excluded from communication. I just don't ever know what's going on," any leader can do something to remedy that issue on their team.

My colleague once said, "I don't avoid difficult conversations; I avoid difficult conversations with people I don't trust." Inherent in all of the strategies we've outlined in this chapter is that these conversations, properly handled, can build trust and actually enhance performance. Listening, responding proactively, and seeking feedback—that's just good leadership.

Chapter 8: Navigate Difficult Conversations
Reflection for Individuals

Having a difficult conversation requires us to be comfortable with the uncomfortable. It starts by saying what you mean and addressing the issue with the facts, what you know to be true. It is about being courageous and having that conversation you have been avoiding or dreading in order to break down barriers to performance. Now, most of us would never dare go into a salary negotiation or job interview unprepared. Yet, we often go into difficult conversations without having planned them or considered what could happen over the course of the dialogue. What follows is a preparation checklist.

Before entering a difficult conversation, walk through these five categories and subpoints. Are you prepared?

1. *Have I created safety?*
   - ☐ Create a safe environment.
   - ☐ Have the conversation privately.
   - ☐ Reflect before speaking.
   - ☐ Assume good intent.

2. *Am I willing to explore?*
   - ☐ Have an attitude of discovery.
   - ☐ Watch body language.
   - ☐ Actively listen.
   - ☐ Ask follow-up questions.
   - ☐ Do not interrupt.
   - ☐ Repeat back what you heard to ensure clarity.
   - ☐ Use reflective statements: "What I hear you saying is . . ." "Is this what you meant when you said . . ."

☐ Share your perspective.

☐ Stick to the facts.

☐ Do not undermine their perspective.

3. *Do I rely on reason and focus?*

☐ State the reason clearly.

☐ Focus on the facts.

☐ Call things what they are.

☐ Share the evidence and impact.

4. *Can I manage emotions effectively?*

☐ Manage emotional energy.

☐ Stay grounded.

☐ Breathe deeply; do not sigh.

☐ Stay calm and encourage them to do so as well.

5. *Is everyone clear on the solution and closure?*

☐ Point out problems; offer solutions.

☐ Acknowledge their suggestions.

☐ Check clarity on solution.

☐ Thank them for speaking with you.

☐ Set a thirty-day check-in meeting.

Capture Your Insights

....

....

....

Chapter 8: Navigate Difficult Conversations
Application for Leaders

As a leader, preparation for a difficult conversation requires additional thought in two key areas, particularly when the dialogue is with a subordinate.

Identify an upcoming difficult conversation. Use the "Reflection for Individuals" activity and the two categories below to guide your conversation. As you converse, be sensitive to the behavior zone the person may be in (Damaging, Limiting, or High-Performance).

☐ **Power.** What comes out of your mouth has additional weight. Without realizing it, you can shut down a conversation before it has even begun. Ensure that you equalize power before the conversation. This might mean meeting in a neutral location instead of your office, sitting side by side instead of behind a desk, and stating outright that the other person's perspective is as important as your own in this conversation.

....

....

....

Capture Your Insights

....

....

....

....

....

☐ **Defense/Persuasion.** Difficult conversations are not a debate. Plan to open with a question that puts the ball in the other person's court and clarifies your intent. For example, "I know you want to talk about the decision that was made last week. My intent is to really listen to your concerns and together build a plan to move forward." Then challenge yourself not to interrupt or rebut any of the other person's comments.

....

....

....

Capture Your Insights

....

....

....

....

....

....

....

....

....

....

....

Life shrinks or expands in
proportion to one's courage.[*]

—Anaïs Nin, author

[*] Anaïs Nin, *The Early Diary of Anaïs Nin*, Vol. 3 (1923–1927). Boston: Houghton Mifflin Harcourt, 1983.

Part 3: Choose Courage

When we bring unconscious biases to the surface, we find they're often not in alignment with our values. But we don't necessarily know what to *do* about that imbalance. As we move through this section, we'll discover four ways to act with courage, along with associated skills and tools you can utilize.

In our framework, identifying bias helps us make progress at the individual level. Cultivating meaningful connection helps us make progress at the interpersonal level. And choosing courage helps us make progress on bias at all levels, particularly in our teams and organizations.

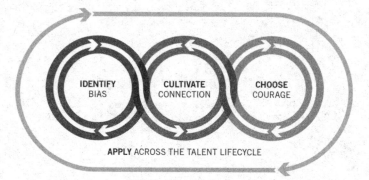

Frame/Reframe

Frame:	Reframe:
If I confront bias, it will just create more division.	When I effectively confront bias, I create a space where all are valued and able to contribute our best.

I'm taken by this word "effective," because depending on how we confront bias, we could create division in the process. But if we can use the skills of identifying, coping, allying, and advocating, we can address bias in a way that enhances—rather than divides—our teams and organizations.

The Principle of Growth

Bias is not a one-shot deal. We won't ever have an exhaustive list of all our biases. Bias will continue to show up—in new circumstances and in ourselves. To grow, we must regularly assess where bias might be showing up and what we can do about it.

Chapter 9: What Is Courage?

Courage isn't absence of fear; it is the awareness that something else is important.

—Stephen R. Covey, bestselling author of *The 7 Habits of Highly Effective People*

A manager leads a successful engineering division working on complex projects for clients. One of his division's more capable engineers has been going through a gender transition to female over the last year. This engineer has been open about her transition, and the manager is respectful when the topic comes up. However, he realizes he hasn't been considering her for the more visible, client-facing projects in the past few months, even though she has successfully led similar projects in the past. It takes **courage to identify** when we might be making decisions based on bias.

Worried about repercussions to his job, a team member doesn't display any photos of his husband in his office or even on the home screen of his phone. Some of his co-workers make homophobic jokes, and a few of the senior leaders laugh along with them. He tries to ignore it, but it's starting to get to him, and if he avoids those colleagues, it will have an impact on his work. He notices a team member who also doesn't find the jokes funny and decides to confide in her over a coffee break one day. He just needs to talk with someone. It takes **courage to cope** with being on the receiving end of bias.

A group of high-ranking women working in the Obama White House noticed they were being talked over and disregarded in important meetings. They decided to team up and amplify one another's voices. When one contributed a good idea that was ignored in a meeting, another woman would bring the idea up again and point out whose idea it was. When a woman's idea was passed over and then brought up by a man, another woman would point out that originally it was the first woman's idea. This practice came to be known as amplification, and became a widespread strategy for allyship. It takes **courage to be an ally.**

In 2006, activist Tarana Burke began using the phrase "Me Too" to raise awareness of the pervasiveness of sexual abuse and assault. The movement didn't begin to spread widely until October 2017, when tens of thousands of people began posting their stories of surviving sexual harassment and assault on social media. It created a movement around the globe to protect victims, educate the workplace on appropriate behavior, and teach people what to do if they experience or witness problematic behavior. It takes **courage to be an advocate.**

Courage comes in many forms. In each of these examples, we can see courage implemented differently.

We define **courage** as the mental or moral strength to strive and persevere in the face of uncertainty, fear, and difficulty. By framing it in four different ways, we allow for the reality of circumstances—there is no one way to respond to difficulty or negativity, no single strategy for shifting from the Limiting or Damaging Zones to the High-Performance Zone.

Think about your earlier examples of times you've been in the Damaging or Limiting Zones. How could courage make a difference in that situation? Would that courage come from you or from another person? How could courage move that situation from damaging or limiting to high performance?

ANNE

Several years ago, I was hosting a group of technology chief information officers and other senior executives over dinner. In attendance were both female and male executives, as well as their guests. We got to talking about talent and the importance of supporting next-generation leaders. The executive sitting next to me by all external measures was a successful, well-known leader who even spent some of his time teaching at a top university. He said, "You know, I've had some amazing young women on my team, but then they get married and have children."

Wait . . . what? Did he really say that? What was additionally surprising was that his wife was sitting right next to him, and he had daughters! I felt I had to speak up. I graciously pressed him on why he felt that amazing women contributors became less amazing after they got married and had kids. He shared his rationale that women who got married and had kids could no longer stay late at work, having to leave early. Their schedules were impacted by the fact that they became mothers.

Well, suffice it to say, we engaged in a very lively debate about his biases (note that I did not use this word with him), and I tried to gracefully reframe his perspective. I asked him why he believed men didn't become less amazing when they got married or became parents—and we had a robust discussion about differences, similarities, communications, and expectations. I'll admit that there was one small moment when I thought there might be some risk in pushing him, as he was a very large client of mine, but I realized it was more important to have courage and engage in the discussion. The good news is that this dialogue did not in any way harm or derail our relationship. Rather, because of its authenticity, it served as a solid foundation for our interactions and growth going forward.

Careful and Bold Courage

Author Mary Anne Radmacher once wrote: "Courage doesn't always roar. Sometimes courage is the quiet voice at the end of the day that says, 'I'll try again tomorrow.'"*

We often think of courage as bold and brash. But it can have an impact without being brazen. Effective courage can be careful or bold, and

---

* Mary Anne Radmacher, *Courage Doesn't Always Roar*. San Francisco: Conari Press, 2009.

by applying a combination of approaches, we can make progress. It's a spectrum, and we might apply courage differently based on the circumstances in which we find ourselves.

Bold courage demands immediate change, action, and progress. **Careful courage** is more appropriate in situations where you may be at risk professionally or personally and where safety is low. And of course there are scenarios that lie somewhere between these two.

Let's think for a moment about that distinction and the four ways to act with courage. If you notice bias in your decision making, for example, is that a time to use careful or bold courage? You might choose careful courage, because you wouldn't want colleagues to irrevocably label your decisions as biased. You might quietly practice some of the tactics recommended under "Courage to Identify"—checking assumptions and learning about the individuals or circumstances about which you are making decisions.

Looking at another example, if you notice that only individuals with certain job functions are being admitted to your organization's leadership-development program, you might use more bold courage to advocate for change. This could include speaking to a senior leader, perhaps even someone on the executive team or the CEO, about your interest in attending this program and employing group strategies such as organizing a learning committee to explore other options available to staff with this interest.

Recently a co-worker and I were discussing an up-and-coming politician I happen to support. The colleague felt that this politician had great intent but talked without thinking and alienated people with her brashness. My colleague then said, "Pamela, you'd make a much better politician because you say things in a way that leaves people open to exploring them." Other work colleagues have said something similar. Part of me thought, "Ouch, that hurts a little," because a huge part of my identity is being a big, booming voice about issues I care about. Was my voice becoming . . . tepid?

With more thought, I realized this feedback was actually an indicator that I was applying the right type of courage in the right context. While my brazen courage is appropriate in many situations, my colleagues' feedback reflected that careful, considerate courage was working in a professional context. That's where we need to make progress, by leaving our echo chambers and communicating effectively with people operating from many different points of view.

What are the strengths and limitations of having careful courage? We can build a foundation of understanding carefully before we go to the other extreme. Careful courage is valuable when we're in risky, uncertain, or volatile situations—or when we simply need to pause and think. In conversations based in the emotional or primitive brain, we can start with careful courage.

ANNE

When I first became an executive, I was in a meeting with my new peer group and several of our team members. Being new to the organization, I didn't have full context for the meeting topic, but my approach in such situations was to demonstrate a balanced amount of curiosity while supporting my team's interests and feeling out the boundaries of my new role. I asked a question about the timelines and release schedule. One tenured VP snapped at me, calling me "silly" for asking such a question. I was furious. But I knew that if I confronted him there, it would not set the right tone for our partnership or for the team.

After the meeting was over, I pulled him aside in a private office and proceeded to tell him why my assertion was not silly, as it was based on my personal experience (which he did not know I had, by the way). I also then proceeded to tell him to never call me or anyone else silly, as it was derogatory and inappropriate, particularly for a senior leader. I remember shaking inside during the whole conversation. I didn't know at the time that my approach was courageous or that my choice of actions demonstrated courage in a subtler fashion as opposed to a more overt way. I'm thankful that, in that situation, I chose the right course of action. As to his response? He listened and was clearly taken aback by my direct feedback and pointed comments. He did not defend his behavior, nor did he apologize for what he said. Well, in this case, our relationship progressed delicately, somewhat on eggshells. We and our teams were able to collaborate. But we never became close.

Personally, I prefer the words "purposeful courage" to "careful courage." Sometimes it takes courage *not* to act or react, because you need to see the forest instead of the trees, and you need to focus on the war, not the immediate battle at hand. Often the courageous act is to let things go for a greater good or purpose—even though, in the moment, it may not seem that way.

MARK

"Careful and bold courage" applies to feedback as well. I've been lucky at FranklinCovey to have worked for several leaders who have empowered me, providing feedback and encouragement with just the right mix of courage and consideration—the courage to be honest about the situation and the consideration to treat me like a human being in the process.

These leaders were able to discern when to use careful courage and when to use bold courage with their feedback, sometimes even in the same conversation. Both types of courage work when the person has first demonstrated their integrity and is transparent with their intent.

For example, I remember one of the first times I presented to an executive group. The FranklinCovey account executive responsible for the client attended the work session as well. The success of this session would determine whether we did any further work with the client. Right off, I could tell I wasn't connecting with the group. They seemed distant and unengaged. I guess it was obvious to my colleague as well.

At the first break, he said to me, in essence, "Mark, don't forget that several of these executives are founders, and they've all known each other for years. They've created something they're very proud of and trust one another's opinions. Their bias is to look internally for solutions. They don't know enough about you to extend you that same trust yet. With this group, rather than sharing what you know right off, you might try having them share what they know first and then build on that."

The energy and engagement in the room changed immediately. The conversations were deeper and richer and more relevant to them. The day ended up being a huge success, all because someone had the courage to give me direct, relevant, timely feedback in a way that didn't belittle or discourage me, but rather empowered me!

Over the next four chapters, you'll read through sixteen different strategies you can use as you encounter bias in the workplace. As you read, note which ones speak to you and work in your context.

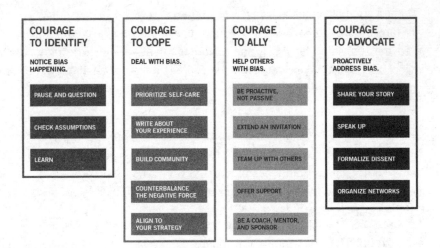

ANNE

I am an avid student of Maya Angelou's work. While much of her writing speaks to me and has helped affirm the way I think professionally, one of my favorite quotes of hers is: "Courage is the most important of all the virtues, because without courage, you can't practice any other virtue consistently."

Pause for a moment. Think of the gravity of this. Yes, you may know what's right. You may believe in equality and equity. You may believe in diversity and inclusion. You may want to create a workplace culture in which all the members of your team feel they belong and thus are performing at their fullest potential—and in this way lifting up the performance of the entire team. But none of this matters if you don't have the courage to *act*. Occasionally you must take action when it's not popular, when it's uncomfortable, and when the consequences are unknown and might even be bad. Courage is action in the face of fear, uncertainty, and doubt. And it's a foundational trait in inclusive and role-model leadership.

Chapter 9: What Is Courage?
Reflection for Individuals

1. What type of courage are you most comfortable with: careful (used when your professional or personal risk is high and your safety is low), or bold (demands immediate action)? How might your courage preference be affecting your workplace experience?

....

....

....

2. What is an example of careful courage you've seen at work?

....

....

....

3. What is an example of bold courage you've seen at work?

....

....

....

4. Has there been a time when you should have applied careful courage instead of bold courage, or vice versa?

....

....

....

Chapter 9: What Is Courage?
Application for Leaders

1. How does a preference for careful or bold courage translate to your team dynamics and decision making? How might that affect how others view your leadership style?

....

....

....

2. Do you tend to recognize and reward team members who display careful courage or bold courage? Why do you think that is?

....

....

....

3. How have you made it safe for your team to display both types of courage when appropriate? What could you do differently?

....

....

....

4. Consider a time when a team member exhibited courage. Knowing what you know now, how might you have responded differently?

....

....

....

Chapter 10: Courage to Identify

The vast majority of our mental processing is happening outside of our conscious awareness, which means we are slipping up and not seeing it sometimes. What happens when the slipup is made visible to us? Do we shut down or do we learn and grow?

—Dolly Chugh, bestselling author and psychologist, New York University Stern School of Business*

Identifying bias is a foundational form of courage underlying the other three types, and in this section, we'll review three additional tools to work with, strategies to identify bias with.

Most people are content to assume they are unbiased and are making rational decisions based on facts and logic. Admitting this is not the case can be disturbing at best. Identifying that we need to improve, slow down, and question our decision making is an act of courage.

ANNE

We must start with ourselves and look deep within to bring our own biases to the surface. And because many of our biases are unconscious, causing us to act automatically, we need to engage others who really know us, people we trust, to give us candid feedback to help us. Once we do this, we can then more effectively broaden our support of others.

---

* Katherine Milkman, "Are You a 'Good-ish' Person? How to Push Past Your Biases." *Knowledge@Wharton,* September 27, 2018; https://knowledge.wharton.upenn.edu/article/reexamining-your-unconscious-biases/.

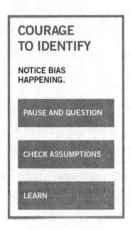

Here are three ways to identify bias in ourselves or others:

Strategy: Pause and Question

Bias happens at the speed of thought. When we take a moment and check our thinking, we can see if biases are impacting our decisions and reactions.

Start by making a habit of pausing before assigning someone a task—both high-stakes projects that can put a career in high gear and smaller tasks that can slow it down. According to the *Harvard Business Review*:

> Women report doing about 20% more "office housework," on average, than their white male counterparts, whether it's literal housework (arranging for lunch or cleaning up after a meeting), administrative tasks (finding a place to meet or prepping a PowerPoint), emotional labor ("He's upset—can you fix it?") or undervalued work (mentoring summer interns). This is especially true in high-status, high-stakes workplaces. Women engineers report a "worker bee" expectation at higher rates than white men do, and women of color report it at higher rates than white women do. Meanwhile, glamour work that leads to networking and promotion opportunities, such as project leadership and presentations, goes disproportionately to white men. When the consultancy GapJumpers analyzed the performance

reviews of a tech company client, it found that women employees were 42% more likely than their male colleagues to be limited to lower-impact projects; as a result, far fewer of them rose
to more-senior roles.*

Think of a time when you acted in a biased way and realized it afterward. What would have helped you catch yourself before you acted?
Here are some tips for creating those pauses moving forward:

- When emotions are high, separate *what* you're feeling and experiencing from *why* you're feeling and experiencing that. Ask:

  - What am I thinking?

  - What am I feeling?

  - Am I being reactive?

  - What's causing my reaction?

- Use the mindfulness practices in Chapter 4 to strengthen your ability to put space between stimulus and response.

- Jot down three occasions in your work routine when you might be
  at risk of falling in the "need for speed" bias trap—perhaps when
  your team is behind on deadlines, when someone quits and you
  don't have a succession plan in place, or when your group is sched-
  uled to travel a lot.

MARK

I've extended this "pause and question" strategy even to my email communication. I've set up a rule that automatically holds all outgoing emails
for a brief period of time before sending. This gives me the chance to
think about what I've sent before the train actually leaves the station.

---

* Joan C. Williams and Sky Mihaylo, "How the Best Bosses Interrupt Bias on
Their Teams." *Harvard Business Review,* November–December 2019; https://hbr
.org/2019/11/how-the-best-bosses-interrupt-bias-on-their-teams.

Strategy: Check Assumptions

Assumptions are beliefs we accept as truth, but they are based on feelings, opinions, and biases. A former client of mine shared her experience being on the receiving end of an ageist assumption: "I'm an active and healthy sixty-year-old woman. I like to think I'm an early adopter and a team player. But it's very noticeable that in marketing strategy meetings, I'm talked over, talked at, or dismissed altogether because I'm not considered to be the 'target demographic' we are trying to reach." The consistent assumption this client expressed, that she had no value to contribute because of her age, put her in the Limiting Zone and robbed the team of the benefit of her experience. As a leader, consider each member of your team and the assumptions you currently hold about them. Do those assumptions impact your decisions or how you react to their ideas? The best leaders are vigilant about challenging faulty assumptions.

One of our manufacturing clients has a best practice around the rooting out of harmful assumptions about others. In a state with 80 percent unemployment for people with cognitive and intellectual disabilities, this firm launched a disability internship program to "break down stereotypes by challenging ourselves to raise our expectations about people with disabilities."

As another example, some leaders assume that gender inequity in the workplace is due to women leaving their professions to care for children. But in an employee-retention study by Catalyst, the two main reasons women cited for leaving their workplaces were a lack of respect and not enough opportunities for advancement.* Challenging assumptions changes how we frame the problem. Understanding the real reason women leave the workplace allows us to create an action plan for addressing that disparity.

Think of a time when someone's opinion or contribution surprised you. How did it differ from the assumption you'd made? What was the impact of your assumption?

---

* Mason Donovan and Mark Kaplan. *The Inclusion Dividend: Why Investing in Diversity & Inclusion Pays Off*. Salisbury, NH: DG Press, 2019.

Here are some questions to ask yourself as you challenge assumptions in future situations:

- What are the facts?

- What am I missing?

- How have I filled the gaps in missing information?

- How can I fill these gaps with facts in the future?

MARK

I learned to speak Spanish fluently when I lived in Argentina, and my accent is pretty good, if I do say so myself. While living there, I tried very hard to culturally assimilate, and yet people always knew I was American.

Several times when I would speak to someone in Spanish, they would reply, "*No hablo inglés*" (I don't speak English). I would then tell them in Spanish that I was speaking Spanish, and they would repeat "*No hablo inglés*"! This could go on for multiple rounds. I know (at least I'm pretty sure) that my Spanish wasn't that bad, plus I was literally speaking Spanish words! But I exuded "American," and some people simply couldn't hear my Spanish. Even the reality of the situation couldn't overcome their assumptions.

Strategy: Learn

"Solving" for bias is not a onetime endeavor but a consistent process of growth paired with the willingness to continue exploring the impact of bias on your life, your organization, and society. We can support this exploration through continuous learning. A healthcare client of ours not only provides unconscious-bias training, but holds follow-up conferences and seminars addressing different components of bias and inclusion annually. This has the effect of making bias an ongoing conversation, rather than something that's addressed once and considered "settled."

Think of a time when you learned something new and it changed your mind about a previously held belief. What helped you change how you saw the situation?

Here are some tips for continuous learning:

- Choose one bias to focus on in yourself. Notice how and when the bias shows up as you engage with others and in your decisions and actions in the next week.

- Commit to staying updated about workplace bias, diversity, or inclusion. Setting up a simple news alert or subscribing to a podcast can push this commitment right to your inbox.

- Head to your various social media accounts and follow a thought leader, a journalist, an author, or an activist with a different perspective from your own. One of the many benefits of social media is that it pulls back the curtain on conversations that might have been off limits to us previously, but are now happening publicly in chats and feeds we're all welcome to view respectfully. When speaking to *The Guardian,* activist and musician Will Butler of Arcade Fire said, "Twitter is a great place to shut up and listen," where you can hear voices you wouldn't normally be able to access outside of social media.*

ANNE

A type of bias that exists in many large organizations is functional bias. I've spent the bulk of my career in sales and in front of customers, so I view others and my work through a market-dominant lens. Replace market in this sentence with any function or role: finance, human resources, marketing, IT, product management, legal, or any other department.

This bias is natural, but in order for the collective business to be successful, leaders and teams across all functions must collaboratively work

---

* Laura Barton, "Arcade Fire: 'People Have Lost the Ability to Even Know What a Joke Is. It's Very Orwellian.'" *The Guardian,* March 30, 2018; https://www .theguardian.com/music/2018/mar/30/arcade-fire-interview.

together. Too often, work groups are too homogeneously formed to come up with an optimal outcome. Cross-functional goal alignment, communications, and governance are often lacking. As a result, fresh and diverse perspectives are not brought to the table.

So what's the answer to this? It's inclusion and engagement. Say you and your team are working on a key project. Take a step back and look at the composition of the team. Does it include a good balance of team members? Is there representation of not only those who are doing the work, but also those who are key to providing input as well as those who will receive the output? Who are your stakeholders? Have you included them in some way in the process—whether it's in the creative stages, the developmental stages, and/or the operational stages of your work? And have you factored in enough time for iteration? In today's world, the market moves fast, and by engaging a broader array of people earlier and throughout the process, you'll by definition be on a stronger path to engagement and buy-in.

Here's a bonus safety tip. Perhaps the most common pushback I've received to engaging more people in anything is the concern that things will take too long and that "there isn't time for that." In reality, if this involvement is handled right, you will actually save time: more people will be "all in" to whatever you're working on because they will have been involved (even if only by giving feedback) throughout. If, on the other hand, this is not done, there will be naysayers and detractors—some of whom will be silent—and they will all serve as speed bumps on your desired smooth path forward. And in the worst of cases, some may actually try to fully derail your efforts and hard work.

The approach doesn't need to be onerous. A couple of things I've done are to include key partners as members of my extended direct-report team—finance, legal, human resources, corporate communications, and more. Also, I'll reach out, ad hoc, to my functional peers from time to time to "give them a heads-up" or to "bounce something off of them" or to "get their guidance" on something. This builds a true partnership, a team culture that serves as the strongest foundation for the success of our business as a whole.

You don't have to be part of a big business to harness this strategy. If you're a small business, you still have stakeholders, especially those in your immediate community. Involve and engage them. You also have peers in the market—you can get insights from them too. Cast your net broadly. Learning, insight, and support can come from anywhere. And most important, be sure to stay in touch with your customers.

Chapter 10: Courage to Identify
Reflection for Individuals

The tools over this and the next three chapters consist of hypothetical scenarios based on real-world experiences. The goal of each scenario is to provide a situation so you can consider how you might respond. Review the strategies introduced in each preceding section and decide which you would feel most comfortable applying in this situation to make progress.

"Courage to Identify" Strategies

- Pause and Question
- Check Assumptions
- Learn

Bias Scenario

You are part of a team working on a cross-functional project. Most of your team is local, with the exception of Maya. She is based in another country, and the difference between your time zones is eight hours. You've struggled to establish a strong rapport with Maya, and your conversations are mostly small talk or focused on work assignments. You don't always understand her accent. It's been hard on team conference calls to understand what she says. You don't want to accidentally say the wrong thing or offend her, and you feel like you could easily and inadvertently say something insensitive.

1. What bias(es) might be at play?

....

....

....

2. How might those bias(es) be affecting your work and Maya's work (Performance Model)?

....

....

....

3. Which "Courage to Identify" strategy would you utilize in this situation, and why?

....

....

....

....

....

....

....

....

....

....

....

....

....

....

Chapter 10: Courage to Identify
Application for Leaders

Bias Scenario

You have three direct reports who are interested in attending your profession's annual conference, but you have only enough in the budget to send one of them.

Direct Report 1 is the youngest on your team but has a lot of potential. She reminds you of yourself at that age.

Direct Report 2 is quiet and reserved. His work seems good so far, but it's been hard to make a connection with him.

Direct Report 3 is the oldest on your team and was interim manager before you were hired. She has been friendly but sometimes pushes back on your decision making.

1. What bias(es) might be at play?

....

....

2. How might those bias(es) be affecting your work and your team's work?

....

....

3. Which "Courage to Identify" strategy would you utilize in this situation, and why?

....

....

Chapter 11: Courage to Cope

*Caring for myself is not self-indulgence, it is self-preservation.**

—Audre Lorde, writer and activist

It is no small thing to be on the receiving end of bias. If you feel like your possibilities are being inhibited and you're in the Limiting or Damaging Zone, research shows that those experiences are detrimental to your overall well-being and have an impact on your ability to contribute, personally and professionally.

Negative bias essentially pushes you out of your own narrative and instead negatively reframes you. For example, a young engineer gets his first job after graduate school. He graduated with honors and was recognized in a national contest for his skill in robotics and engineering. He was born and raised in Vietnam and came to Canada for college. He speaks heavily accented English, and his new manager and team immediately focus on his accent, consistently making comments about how hard he is to understand. One colleague goes so far as to ask him to contribute to the weekly virtual team meeting in the chat instead of talking. "Just type it in," she says. "It's not worth wasting your breath to talk when we can't understand you anyway."

It takes courage to acknowledge how limiting and ultimately damaging it is to be on the receiving end of bias and to work through that negativity to recenter yourself. Prioritizing self-care, including writing

---

* Audre Lorde. *A Burst of Light and Other Essays,* reprinted. New York: Ixia Press, 2017, 130.

about your experience, building community, finding a counterbalancing influence, and aligning to your strategy are all strategies to support re-centering yourself.

ANNE

In the early part of my career, I was treated differently as a young woman in the workforce. I don't think that it was intentional in many cases, or necessarily malicious, but people had biases nonetheless.

I'll give you an example. One of my very first team jobs was managing a large, geographically dispersed workforce responsible for the operations of one of our service lines. I was half the age of most of the employees. I remember doing an employee session with a group of my front-line technicians. They said, "We know your kind. You're one of those fast-trackers. You're going to be gone in six months." It was clear they didn't want to hear anything I had to say, because they felt that I was there only for a check mark. I told them that I was committed to supporting them and learning from them, and that I intended to be there for much longer than six months. My tenure in that role lasted for three years. Over that period of time, I slowly and steadily earned their trust and respect, and together, we made big progress in serving our customers and improving our customer-care processes.

What I realized early on was that success as a leader was not so much about what you think of your role, but rather about a full understanding of what others believe about you. If you don't consciously think through and work to expose those biases, progress will be hampered. Your team must believe in you and your collective mission. But in order to do so, we must bring to the surface and work through biases that perhaps are shaped by our appearance, others' experiences, hearsay, speculation, a lack of understanding, or some other factor. No doubt, there are challenges like this that each of us has run into—where someone else has assumed something about us that isn't actually true. I've found that not taking yourself too seriously and having a good sense of humor are helpful when working through these types of situations. If you take everything personally, your emotions may get the better of you and you may miss the opportunity for a learning moment, whether for yourself or for others.

Strategy: Prioritize Self-Care

I recently read a meme on social media that proclaimed "self-care is a revolutionary act." (It stuck with me because all knowledge worth remembering can now be distilled in a meme!) The word "self-care" makes many of us think of relaxing spa days and the catharsis of a shopping trip, but the term actually has its roots in activism and was written about extensively in Audre Lorde's 1988 book, *A Burst of Light*. In her definition, self-care meant prioritizing your recovery after you courageously supported equity or justice. Just as you might recover from a strenuous workout with a cooldown stretch, you should prioritize self-care when facing the strain of bias.

Gone are the days when we were expected to "tough it out" or "grin and bear it" in response to poor treatment.

MARK

I like the idea that "self-care is a revolutionary act." A revolutionary act of self-care can be something bold and dramatic or something calculated over time to create change.

Think back to the ideas of careful courage and bold courage. I believe we can practice careful or bold self-care as well. If we're in a contentious or toxic meeting, for example, we might practice bold self-care by speaking up or leaving the room. We might practice careful self-care by taking a few breaths, pausing before we react, then de-stressing after the meeting concludes.

Being the subject of bias or seeing it have an impact on others can take a toll on well-being, often known as an emotional tax (introduced in Chapter 5). After experiencing bias, the number-one skill here is to prioritize self-care. Make sure you're okay. Step away and effectively deal with any associated stress or emotional distress. Self-care can include removing yourself from a situation, meditation, physical activity, journaling, a conversation with a trusted friend, and self-reflection.

In some cases, like the global protests during the summer of 2020 around racial injustice and inclusion, coping with bias can be less about an individual circumstance or incident and more about the influence of organization-wide or societal forces. As the protests raged, Black employees all across the United States and the globe reported they'd never talked so much about race at work. This included internal conversations in Black employee-resource groups, but also extensive outreach from White colleagues to explain their experience with racial injustice or bias at work. While much of this outreach was well-intentioned, as American writer and professor Roxane Gay has said, "Oftentimes we represent not only us but everyone who looks like us," which can invoke its own type of fatigue. Excessive questions about how you are different as a result of any facet of your identity can also push you to the outskirts of your own narrative. Self-care can also mean setting appropriate boundaries with colleagues and leaders in discussing sensitive issues by pushing them to outside resources to answer their questions and refocusing conversations on work deliverables.

In the workplace, organizations can support policies and workplace wellness programs that allow employees to step away and distance themselves from the situation. For example, a federal contracting firm has allocated what they call "focus rooms," small conference rooms for individuals to move into when they need time alone. The company also provides standing and treadmill desks and offers a wellness program for fitness courses, all avenues that support overall employee well-being and can also support coping with bias. At an HR conference for the UN System last year, wellness programming highlights included several enterprise-wide subscriptions to online healthcare companies like Headspace for building a meditation practice, Talkspace for online therapy, and competitive activity apps that promote standing and movement throughout the day.

Think of a time when you were in the Damaging Zone and struggling with the biased behavior of others. What could you have done to take the space and time you needed to recover?

While apps and online platforms can prove helpful, here are some strategies you can implement independent of technology:

- Build moments in your day to break away from your desk or office, from taking a walk to meeting a colleague for coffee.

- Ensure that you aren't allowing the workday to creep into your personal time. Checking emails while at the dinner table or filling the evening's conversation with complaints about work can make it seem like the problems you're facing are all-consuming. Use that time to play a trivia game with your family, or implement your own version of the "Dallas Stack" that Mark mentioned on page 00.

- Consider routines outside of work hours. Self-Care Saturdays might sound trite, but having something to look forward to all week can be incredibly helpful.

Strategy: Write About Your Experience

We each have our own stories about our identity and biases. Noting our experiences in writing can help us understand ourselves and be its own form of self-care.

Writing can feel like a high bar; you might feel that you must have a thought-out plot and purpose to the story you're telling. But the purpose of writing to cope with bias is not about perfection or even about the skill of writing itself. We sometimes need to get out of our head about writing. As I think about my own journey to write about my experiences and stories, a few simple strategies have served me well:

- Look for inspiration. One of my good friends, Elizabeth Acevedo, is an award-winning author of young-adult fiction. One of her strategies to overcome writer's block is to read more. When we read other people's stories, it prompts the emotional part of our brains, which seeks similarity. It can often inspire us to share a story of our own or enable us to cast a different light on an experience we've had. Spend some time perusing *Humans of New York* or similar websites for inspiration on the power of story not only to help us cope, but also to enable us to make change.

• Give yourself permission to be informal. Writing and journaling can come in whatever format is most comfortable to you—prose, verse, bulleted list, or even doodle. What you write doesn't need to be perfectly phrased or punctuated, just captured on the page.

Strategy: Build Community

We've already talked about how isolating it can feel to be on the receiving end of bias. Coping with bias requires we build a community where we are at the center. This community can take many forms. In Chapter 7, I mentioned being part of a book club of professional Black women. While we certainly read and discussed books each month, we also built a community that centered around our experiences in the professional world. We would share stories of being minimized by colleagues or describe instances of noninclusive communications. Employee-resource groups at your organization or fraternal organizations in your community can also serve this purpose.

Sometimes the ways in which we build community begin as something that fulfills a personal need and grows into something that builds community across an even broader group. For example, in August of 2018, Zach Nunn, a senior strategist at a global consulting firm, founded Living Corporate in an effort to build community. He describes how this came to be:

As a first-generation professional who also happens to be a Black man in a predominantly White environment, I asked myself, "What does it look like to create space where marginalized professionals can get practical insight to thrive at work?" That's where the idea of creating a digital media platform that took the whispered points of meaningful advice Black and Brown people infrequently receive and have them "out loud," called Living Corporate.

In a couple of short years, we have had 200 podcasts, dozens of blogs, and multiple webinars where we have featured Black and Brown Fortune 500 leaders, activists, authors, professors, creatives, elected officials, entrepreneurs, and influencers—all of them centering the perspectives of marginalized people at work (e.g., Black, Brown, LGBTQIA+, trans/non-binary, people with disabilities). We have had discussions about how to better advocate for women at work, the challenges of being a first-generation American in the workplace, the experience of being an East Asian at work, the intersectionality of race and sexual orientation, and being a person of color in the C-suite.

Centering these experiences and perspectives by having "real talk" with so many people has been incredible. Getting emails, LinkedIn messages, and social media direct messages of folks often on the periphery that share how being seen through this content gives them the courage to advocate for themselves and "cope" has been incredibly rewarding.

Resources like Living Corporate can ensure that building community is possible regardless of the makeup of your personal network.

ANNE

Emotional tax is real. Even though outside events are spurring our turmoil, the emotions they spark can be hard to dismiss. However, fear, uncertainty, doubt, anger, worry, and jealousy are largely unproductive emotions. It's important to have a support system of people with whom you can talk through challenges and work through issues, so that your emotions don't overwhelm your focus. Bearing the burden of this tax on your own can be overwhelming and lonely, so seek connection where you can find it, and in turn, help others connect as well.

Strategy: Counterbalance the Negative Force

A challenge of being on the receiving end of bias—from racism to ageism to our status as the only administrator on a team of designers—is that it can lead to self-limiting beliefs. We start to see ourselves through a distorted lens. Instead of seeing ourselves as capable, smart, hardworking, and worthy of recognition, we see ourselves as out of place, less than, and unlikely to succeed. But coping with these feelings doesn't have to be a solitary activity. In fact, struggling alone can often heighten these less-than-ideal sentiments. Find a counterbalancing presence in your life. What do I mean by a counterbalance? For me, a counterbalancing force has two facets. First, they know you well. Second, they have a perspective different from your own. The counterbalancing force in my life is my husband. When I'm on the receiving end of bias, my tendency is to get wrapped up in the injustice of it all and charge headfirst into conflict to defend myself. My husband knows me well enough to know that, and coaches me on how to be more measured and proactive in my response to bias. This has served me over the course of my career.

If you don't already have a counterbalancing force in your life—a confidant, as we described in Chapter 7—you may decide to fill this role with a coach or a mentor. It is in moments of difficulty that our network can have the most significant impact. Is there someone you already know who could become a formal mentor for you? If not, once you have a better understanding of the biases limiting you and/or others, find a mentor who can provide a fresh perspective. Start with local organizations or online platforms like LinkedIn.com and Meetup.com and expand outside your comfort zone. Keep an eye out for people who inspire you.

Coaches and mentors give us the gift of their experience. They can share lessons about how they have recognized and coped with bias in their lives. For example, at one of our university clients, many personnel—in particular, staff members of color in frontline roles—were feeling disconnected from the university and unsupported in their professional development. The university set up a yearlong no-cost mentoring program matching mentor and mentee across demographic profiles and professional roles for maximum growth.

Think of a coach or mentor in your life who helped you deal with a difficult situation. How did they help you? Could you do the same for someone else?

Finding a coach or mentor is a best practice in many arenas—dealing with bias, building your career, transitioning careers, and generally getting better. But it's certainly easier said than done. If you currently have a coach or mentor (ideally, you have both!):

- Reach out to them through this lens of bias. Do you feel like you're on the receiving end of bias? Share your story with your coach and/or mentor and get their insights on how you can best cope with and navigate this situation. If you currently don't have a coach or mentor, think about who you do know that could fill this role.

- Is there a person in your network from whom you'd like to learn or whose insights you value?

- Think about the nature of your current relationship with this person. Do they know who you are? Have you engaged with them before formally or informally? If the answer to both of these questions is yes, reach out for an exploratory conversation.

- Keep in mind that many leaders are receiving more requests for mentoring than their schedules will allow, and that a good mentoring or coaching relationship is built on a solid foundation of trust. Email or call for a preliminary conversation. Ask if a larger mentoring relationship is of interest or if they could spend an hour or so with you exploring a specific problem. Many leaders are happy to engage for an hour initially as opposed to the pressure of a long-term relationship. And that initial interaction can lead to something more substantive down the road.

- Be open to their perspective and vulnerable in what you share.

Finally, if you don't have prospects for a mentor, consider engaging a paid coach. A survey of your network, a conversation with HR, or a search on LinkedIn will likely yield a plethora of certified-coach options you can engage.

> **ANNE**
>
> Surround yourself with coaches, mentors, friends, and sponsors who lift you up, make you better, and push you in a positive way. Surround yourself with people who are different from you, challenge you, and stretch you. Most important, surround yourself with people who will catch you if you fall and who will ensure that you get back up and push forward.
>
> And I'd ask that you also purposefully be that for others. This is how we continue to make progress. Together we are better.

Strategy: Align to Your Strategy

Immediate reactions can come from the primitive or emotional parts of the brain. When we react to situations hastily, our responses can be impulsive—and often damaging. When we are proactive, we choose a better response, moving into the thinking brain.

Organizationally and interpersonally, people usually expect a response immediately in conversations or meetings. To the extent you can, build a new cultural norm that allows you to receive information and then say, "Let me get back to you tomorrow with a response." Build in time to consider the strategic response.

Think of a time when you said or did something you regretted afterward. What were the consequences? If you could revisit that situation, what would you say or do differently? Coping with bias in a reactive way can be detrimental to your own professional opportunities. I was discussing bias with a colleague recently, and she shared that she'd had several really negative employment experiences with bias, times when she lost professional opportunities as a result of bias. She said that as she looked back over her career, she was more successful than anyone who had limited her possibilities. She didn't say this in a callous way, nor did she wish them ill will. Her larger point was that regardless of the experiences she'd had at work and the harm that being on the receiving end of bias had had on her emotional well-being and her ability to contribute, she worked to continuously respond in alignment with her strategy. By creating some space between the instances of bias and her response to them, she was able to prioritize her desired professional trajectory.

So much of proactively choosing a response is about being in touch with the emotions the situation is generating in you. What follows is a quick thought path to proactively choose a response and ensure you are aligned to your professional goals:

- First, ask yourself: What emotion am I feeling about this?

- Then, ask: What is my professional goal here? Do I want to get more visibility or support for this project? Do I want to be seen as a collaborative colleague? Is this the moment to speak up?

- Next, ask: What would the most constructive response to this circumstance be that would support the goal?

- Then, spend some time planning what you can do or say proactively. Based on the complexity of the situation, this can be two to five minutes at your desk jotting down some notes, or a larger strategy session with a trusted friend or coach.

- Finally, practice the response to refine it and implement it in conversation.

A Final Note: If Nothing Changes

Sometimes we deploy all these strategies to cope with bias, yet nothing happens in our external circumstances. We've done everything we can think of to make progress, but we're still in the Limiting or Damaging Zone.

At that point, we must make a decision. We owe it to ourselves to leave harmful circumstances, if at all possible. Organizations increasingly realize that if they don't create an inclusive, equitable environment, they will not retain their people or customers. So I would encourage you to vote with your feet and take the steps necessary to find a workplace that values your contribution, if that's an option for you.

Chapter 11: Courage to Cope
Reflection for Individuals

"Courage to Cope" Strategies

- Prioritize Self-Care

- Write About Your Experience

- Build Community

- Counterbalance the Negative Force

- Align to Your Strategy

Bias Scenario

You're approaching retirement, and you have a new young manager who is highly educated and driven to get results. But he sometimes seems to make assumptions about the older employees on the team. For example, you like to develop apps in your free time. You recently approached your manager about recommendations for your company's new app. He tells you, "That's okay, Antonio's just out of college and is more familiar with that sort of thing."

The next day, mustering a bit of courage, you share your feelings with your manager and invite him to reconsider your request. Unfortunately, your manager looks annoyed and replies, "Look, I don't want to make a big deal out of this. I've made my decision and I need you to just accept it." Disheartened and feeling unmotivated, you return to your workstation and stare at the retirement date circled on your calendar.

1. What bias(es) might be in play?

....

....

....

2. How might those bias(es) impact your work (Performance Model)?

....

....

....

3. Which "Courage to Cope" strategy might you employ, and why?

....

....

....

....

....

....

....

....

....

....

....

....

....

....

....

Chapter 11: Courage to Cope
Application for Leaders

Bias Scenario

You observe some specific dietary restrictions as part of your religious beliefs. You lead a team in the hospitality industry, where sharing meals as a staff is an important part of the culture. Your team is starting to take liberties with your dietary restrictions and becoming flippant about how "inconvenient" it is to accommodate them. At first, you try to defuse the situation with some levity and, of course, appreciation, but their hostility seems to be increasing. As the leader, you know you have authority, but it doesn't seem appropriate to reprimand them for your own religious accommodation. It's weighing on you that your team doesn't seem to value this part of your identity, but you feel stuck trying to do anything about it.

1. What bias(es) might be in play?

....

....

2. How might those bias(es) impact your work or the team's (Performance Model)?

....

....

3. Which "Courage to Cope" strategy would you utilize in this situation, and why?

....

....

Chapter 12: Courage to Be an Ally

Ally is not a noun. Allies are defined by their actions.

—Dr. Makini King, director of diversity and inclusion initiatives, University of Missouri–Kansas City*

It is natural to react and respond when you are in harm's way. Taking action about something that does *not* impact you directly is something different altogether. It's counterintuitive and unnatural to throw ourselves into the fray of something that doesn't have a direct impact on us.

Being an ally, lending our voices in defense of others, is a courageous act. Understanding others' experiences and offering support can make a world of difference with issues like the emotional tax we mentioned earlier.

An ally is not "I feel so bad about this that I'm going to help you." It's not about anger, resentment, guilt, shame, or pity. Allies understand that addressing unconscious bias is critical to morale and business imperatives, especially when they are in positions of relative power compared to those on the receiving end of bias.

"Privilege" is a trigger word for a lot of people around this topic, because they think it somehow negates their personal effort and accomplishments: "Privilege? Do you know how hard I worked to get here? Do you think I just magically floated into this position?" That's not what privilege is about.

---

* Makini King, "Ally Is Not a Noun." University of Missouri–Kansas City, May 15, 2018. https://info.umkc.edu/diversity/ally-is-not-a-noun/.

Let's think of a metaphorical marathon. Everyone who finishes the marathon accomplished something difficult. But if you finished the marathon with a prosthesis, you overcame barriers I didn't have as an able-bodied person. Having privilege doesn't negate my accomplishment, but it does acknowledge that we were facing a spectrum of different barriers, some subtle and others severe.

Each of us has privilege (and disadvantage) in one form or another. I may not have privilege based on my race or gender, but I do have privilege from being married to a man, holding an advanced degree, and owning my home. Another way to think about this is in alignment with the Performance Model. As a Black woman in corporate America, I am accustomed to being the only person who looks like me in a room, which can mean I walk into the room in the Limiting Zone, feeling like I do not belong because I don't see anyone else like me. And there are many identifiers about which this can be said—for example, the only woman in the room or the only person of color, the only veteran or the only person with a disability. When you are part of the majority in the workplace, that represents privilege, a signaling that you belong there. When you have relative privilege in a circumstance, that's the time to be an ally.

A perfect example is the producing trifecta of Gloria Calderón Kellett, Norman Lear, and Mike Royce. On their hit show *One Day at a Time,* a remake of the original 1975 show featuring a Cuban American family in Los Angeles, Lear and Royce served as key allies to Calderón Kellett, one of the few women of color showrunners in the business. (A showrunner is the most senior producer and highest-ranking person on a television series—91 percent of them are White, and 80 percent are male.*) In their first season, cast and crew would go to the male showrunners with questions and decisions. Lear and Royce consistently redirected them to Calderón Kellett. "The importance of White male allies is no joke," she said. "It changed the game. By Season Two, people were just asking me."

Lear and Royce later advocated for Calderón Kellett when she

---

* Darnell Hunt, "Race in the Writers' Room." *Color of Change,* October 2017; https://hollywood.colorofchange.org/writers-room-report/.

wanted to move into directing. She became the first Cuban American female to direct a multicam television show.

As she became more successful, Calderón Kellett paid it forward by becoming an ally for others. "I've also had to acknowledge my own privileges. I'm very White passing. . . . I talk without an accent. Also, my access to education has been incredible. I have my own personal privileges that I come into this with, so I have to acknowledge those and say, 'How can I then open doors for others?'"

Instead of leaving that a vague aspiration, she decided to create practical resources to help burgeoning filmmakers develop their craft, saying, "Access to tools should not be a privileged thing." She teamed up with BuzzFeed and YouTube to create a free master class, "Hollywood 101," to cover the basics of breaking into the business, and she released the pilot script of *One Day at a Time* so students could study storytelling techniques. She also mentored two up-and-coming Latina directors, Stephanie Beatriz and Melissa Fumero, who both went on to direct episodes of *Brooklyn Nine-Nine*. "I signed both of their DGA [Directors Guild of America] cards," she said. "The signing of it felt significant."[*]

When you sponsor someone, you use your position of power in an organization to build their influence. In a sales context, sales managers are brought in when their relative seniority will help close the sale. When does a customer-service rep call in their manager? When they need some authority, some privilege, in the conversation to keep the customer happy.

Privilege, if we think of it in that way, is asking, "Where do I have relative seniority or advantage?" then using that influence to lift up others, to be an ally by acting proactively, extending an invitation, teaming up with others, offering support, and serving as a coach, mentor, and sponsor. Just as coping with bias is focused on recentering yourself in your narrative, there is some nuance to being an effective ally. Effective allies do not overtake the voices and experiences of those they are working to support. Instead, they work to de-center themselves, ensuring the focus

---

[*] Roxane Gay and Dr. Tressie McMillan Cottom, "The Golden Era." Audio podcast. *Hear to Slay*. Luminary, June 4, 2019.

is not on their fear, guilt, or pain but on making progress for those they are allied with.

Strategy: Be Proactive, Not Passive

As the opening quote to this chapter highlights, the role of an ally is a proactive one. This is an important shift in mindset. If asked directly, many leaders would say they believe in building an inclusive environment, but an ally is not passive in their support. This means they embrace all of the strategies in Chapter 10, "Courage to Identify," and approach allyship with a focus on introspection and learning. A true ally does not wait to be asked but simply takes on the challenge of inequity, standing up to make a positive change.

Strategy: Extend an Invitation

Use your access to invite more people of diverse perspectives to the table. As Kathryn Finney, CEO of Genius Guild, puts it:

> I think there's a disproportionate amount of responsibility on
> the person seeking opportunities versus those in a position to

create opportunities. I recently told a friend, who happens to be a young, prominent White male in tech, "Look, you get invited into rooms that people who look like me will *never* be invited into. The next time you're invited to a 'tech bro' dinner where you know there will be no diversity, just invite someone who does not look like you to join you. And introduce that person to everyone there as someone you endorse and believe is the future of tech. It's very simple." More than any woman or Black person in tech, he has the power to reach out and give someone who is "different from him" a boost. And that boost is free. It's time more power players do their part to diversify the rooms they're in and the tables they're at. It's just good business sense.

Here are some strategies for extending an invitation:

- The next time you attend a conference, panel, or event, invite one of your mentees or someone who might not have otherwise had the opportunity to benefit from that learning.

- If you're invited to be a keynote speaker or other high-profile role, inquire about the diversity of the lineup. If it's lacking, consider suggesting an alternate speaker who might add to the diversity of perspectives.

- Many organizations have cross-functional teams assigned to high-profile projects. If you're tapped to sit in on a new team or project, think about how other perspectives can be brought to that project, formally or informally.

Strategy: Team Up with Others

Making progress on bias doesn't have to be labor or work that you do by yourself. If this is something you have strong feelings about, chances are others do as well. Teaming up with others can mean building a coalition of other allies or amplifying the work of marginalized groups by lending your privilege and voice to their cause. Team up with others to learn more about your own bias and theirs, explore bias in your organization or community, and align your voices with those who are disproportionately impacted by bias.

Research shows that when those from marginalized groups speak up about issues of inclusion, it hurts them over the course of their careers, and when members of the majority group speak up for inclusion, their careers benefit. Given this pattern, an intelligence agency has a best practice around their employee-resource groups—each group must have an executive sponsor who is not a member of the group. This practice ensures that the burden of advocating falls to the executive sponsor rather than to members of the employee-resource group.

- Think of a time you were part of a group that had an impact by teaming up.

- Think about a bias that does not have a direct impact on you, but you see it impacting others in your organization or community.

- Are there others who see this impact?

- Consider how you can reach out to them to collaborate on solutions.

Strategy: Offer Support

Think back to the idea of careful or bold courage. Being an ally is not always about a big, loud gesture. It is often incredibly meaningful for those experiencing bias to know they have the support of a friend or colleague who will listen to them, support them, and give them a place to vent.

People who are coping with bias need to have a safe space to communicate. If you can offer support as a friend or trusted ally, that can make all the difference for people, depending on what they're experiencing. Remember that while you might also have strong emotions about the circumstance, allyship is not about your own emotions but instead about making space to center the emotions of those you are allied with.

Think of a time when a colleague was struggling with something. Did you offer support? If not, what held you back? If so, how did that feel?

Here are some tips for effectively offering support:

- Observe and acknowledge when people seem to be experiencing big feelings.

- Listen to and acknowledge others' ideas.

- Begin by listening to understand, not to resolve.

- Act as a thinking partner to brainstorm ways to address bias.

MARK

I'm alive today because of an ally offering support. I was living in Virginia in 1993 when, at the age of thirty-three, I finally came to the realization that being gay was not a phase or something I would eventually grow out of. Facing that reality shook me to my core. I became severely depressed and spent a couple of weeks locked away in my bedroom with blankets covering all the windows. My depression got progressively worse until one day I decided I couldn't live with it anymore. So I made the decision not to . . . live anymore.

I had everything planned out to look like an accident so I wouldn't bring shame on myself or my family. The night before what was to be my final day, I decided I needed to tell someone, anyone. I called my brother. He was living in Dallas at the time. When I called, he picked up and said it was lucky I called when I did, because he had left to go camping, forgotten something, and just come back into the house. I blurted out, "I'm gay." I think it totally caught him off guard, because all he could muster was "No, you're not." I told him I really was. After a couple of rounds of back-and-forth, when the reality finally started to settle in with him, his next words saved my life. All he said was "Do you want me to fly there or do you want to fly here?" I immediately left for the airport and flew to Dallas.

Those few simple words said without judgment saved my life. It often doesn't take large acts of courage to make a difference in people's lives. It's amazing the impact a few simple words of support said with sincerity can have!

We all have our own life story. Mine is no more or less significant than anyone else's. There is so much more to people than what we see on the surface. So much can be learned when we seek to understand others' stories and have the courage to share our own.

In the words attributed to Ian Maclaren: "Be kind, for everyone you meet is fighting a hard battle."

Strategy: Be a Coach, Mentor, and Sponsor

The research is clear: bias can have significant impact on a person's personal and professional success. Mentorship, sponsorship, and coaching can most assuredly help people overcome negative bias in their careers. (Refer to Chapter 7, "Tap Into the Power of Networks," for more details on the difference between coaching, mentoring, and sponsoring.) Consider offering your skills and perspective in this way, through informal or formal channels.

For example, a multinational financial institution noticed that women were not being promoted to the senior ranks. They began a coaching initiative, first training all senior management on the importance of building a culture of coaching, then facilitating pairings of coachee and coach between high-potential women and senior officials at the bank.

I'd like to highlight sponsorship in particular. While mentoring and coaching may cost you time, sponsorship is the highest-stakes endeavor of the three because it requires utilizing some of your own political capital to advance others. There is some risk in doing that, and the risk makes sponsorship harder to come by than mentorship or coaching. Herminia Ibarra, a professor of organizational development at London Business School, put it this way: "When it comes to this important distinction, the evidence is also clear: women tend to be over-mentored and under-sponsored."* This reality exists across race and disability as well. While mentoring can build skill and coaching is focused on career strategy, it is sponsorship that can really accelerate promotion, addressing the deep gaps in diversity at the senior ranks of most organizations around the globe.

Think of your last big professional accomplishment. Who was integral in helping or supporting you to achieve that? Is there someone you currently know or work with who would benefit from your experience?

---

* Herminia Ibarra, "A Lack of Sponsorship Is Keeping Women from Advancing into Leadership." *Harvard Business Review,* August 19, 2019; https://hbr.org/2019/08 /a-lack-of-sponsorship-is-keeping-women-from-advancing-into-leadership.

Here are some tips for becoming a coach, mentor, or sponsor:

- Ask questions of those around you about their professional goals.

- Ask what is holding them back.

- Share your experience as appropriate.

- Provide feedback and guidance.

- Consider where you have the political capital to elevate someone else.

- Seek permission from the recipient to serve in any of these roles.

ANNE

When I was named the CEO of AT&T Business, it was very clear to me that many people were advocating for my promotion. I've benefited from allies throughout my career, and as the first woman of color CEO in AT&T history, I have a responsibility to pay it forward. I've spent much of my professional tenure working to serve as an ally to as many people as possible. Here's my advice on how to go about being an effective ally for marginalized people:

- One way to get started as an ally is to **join a group**, whether it's an employee network, an employee-resource group, or outside organizations that focus on a certain demographic, culture, orientation, or religion—even if you don't represent that demographic yourself. I encourage men to join the Women of AT&T, AT&T Women of Business, and other groups; everyone is included if they want to be. It's awesome for people to want to participate in something unfamiliar and perhaps even uncomfortable. This is how we grow.

- I would also reinforce the idea of **challenging your inner cadre**. As you think about joining an organization, surround yourself very purposefully with other perspectives. Pick up some mentees who are different from you, specifically to learn from each other. Both of you can become more informed and experience growth from the relationship.

- A call to action for every leader who wants to be a productive ally: **Sponsor marginalized people**. If you're already mentoring two high-potential people, find two more. Use each of your hands, reach to your side, reach back, and pull a couple more people forward. Finding the greatness in others and helping them fulfill their potential brings joy like no other. Do not underestimate the profound impact you can have on someone.

- Another key step is to **engage**. If you see bias—or feel bias in yourself—engage. If you're not sure, ask. Have courage. Whether it's how you shape your team, how you run your governance, how you celebrate success—widen your net and engage more broadly and more deeply with others. It's okay to feel uncomfortable; in fact, if you're feeling uncomfortable, that's a good thing, because it's a sign that you're pushing against your "norms" and your "status quo." But don't just keep that feeling internalized. Take some action. No matter how small—just do something to move forward, whether it's to develop your own understanding and perspective or to help another person do the same.

- **Speak up**. One of the biggest pieces of advice that I give folks on this topic is to amplify others' voices. If you're in a meeting and realize that someone is the only woman/person of color/young person in the room, notice if they're being spoken over or if their ideas are being co-opted. Being the only of anything is very difficult. And biases, unconscious or otherwise, become even more amplified in the case of "the only." I would also venture to say that each of us has been "the only" at least once in our careers, whether we were the youngest in the room, the only female, the only LGBTQ+ person, the only unmarried person, the only one with no kids, or the only person of color. Use your own stature to elevate the voices of "the only." And take action to ensure that "only" is just a temporary situation.

Chapter 12: Courage to Be an Ally
Reflection for Individuals

"Courage to Be an Ally" Strategies

- Be Proactive, Not Passive

- Extend an Invitation

- Team Up with Others

- Offer Support

- Be a Coach, Mentor, and Sponsor

Bias Scenario

You're a federal employee and your department is about to kick off a project involving your city's traditionally underserved urban areas. You've been with this department for only six months, and you're still learning the ropes. In your 1-on-1, you ask your manager about who she thinks will manage this high-profile project. She says, "I think Keisha is a great fit for this project. She speaks the language of that community."

Keisha has expressed to you that her real interest is in tech and policies that support smart cities. As the only Black employee in the office, she feels pressure to accept projects in urban areas and Black communities, and worries she isn't gaining experience in the area she is passionate about.

1. What bias(es) might be in play?

....

....

....

....

2. How might those bias(es) impact Keisha's work (Performance Model)?

....

....

....

....

3. Which "Courage to Be an Ally" strategy would you utilize in this situation, and why?

....

....

....

....

....

....

....

....

....

....

....

....

....

....

Chapter 12: Courage to Be an Ally
Application for Leaders

Bias Scenario

Your organization is rolling out a mentorship program (Be a Coach or Mentor). You have been matched to three possible mentees:

Mentee 1 is part of a traditionally marginalized group in your organization that you're eager to support. You come from very different backgrounds, and you're a little worried your interactions may be awkward.

Mentee 2 is new to the organization and has been vocal in comparing your organization's processes to those of her former employers. You think she's probably right in some cases, but you're concerned about her approach.

Mentee 3 is from a younger generation. She is one of the top individual contributors in her division, but she's said she's not interested in leadership.

1. Who do you choose and why?

....

....

2. What bias(es) might be in play?

....

....

3. How could you reduce bias in your decision-making process?

....

....

....

Chapter 13: Courage to Be an Advocate

Here in America we are descended in blood and in spirit from revolutionists and rebels—men and women who dared to dissent from accepted doctrine. As their heirs, may we never confuse honest dissent with disloyal subversion.

—Dwight D. Eisenhower, former U.S. president

Advocating is perhaps what we would think of as more traditional courage: the courage to be the squeakiest of wheels to make progress on a large scale.

An interesting example is the CEO Action for Diversity & Inclusion, the largest CEO-driven business commitment to advance diversity and inclusion within the workplace. In their own words, "This commitment is driven by a realization that addressing diversity and inclusion is not a competitive issue, but a societal issue. Recognizing that change starts at the executive level, more than 900 CEOs of the world's leading companies and business organizations are leveraging their individual and collective voices to advance diversity and inclusion in the workplace." The associated website also allows individuals to make pledges and commitments around diversity and inclusion.

This commitment is worth noting because it puts the onus on CEOs rather than on their employees. We must not put the burden of mitigating unconscious bias on its recipients. A study published by the *Academy of Management Journal* found that women and non-White leaders who advocated for diversity initiatives were penalized on their competence and performance ratings.* Let's all step up to advocate for these changes.

---

* David R. Hekman et al., "Does Diversity-Valuing Behavior Result in Diminished Performance Ratings for Non-White and Female Leaders?" *Academy of Management Journal* 60, no. 2 (March 3, 2016); https://doi.org/10.5465/amj.2014.0538.

COURAGE TO ADVOCATE

PROACTIVELY ADDRESS BIAS.

SHARE YOUR STORY

SPEAK UP

FORMALIZE DISSENT

ORGANIZE NETWORKS

Strategy: Share Your Story

We discussed a strategy in Chapter 11 about how writing your story can help you cope with bias. Sharing your story on a large scale could help drive change institutionally. Many people don't understand the impact of bias—your experience might help them get a fuller picture.

"What Does My Headscarf Mean to You?," a TED talk by Yassmin Abdel-Magied, has been viewed more than two million times and translated into more than thirty-one languages at the time of this writing.* Abdel-Magied shares her experience as an immigrant, an engineer, a Muslim, and a woman. The hundreds of comments on the video show discussions that likely would not have happened otherwise, and Yassmin subsequently won a Young Australian of the Year award based on this first step, sharing her story.

All the TED talks, podcasts, articles, blog posts, bits of research, and books written about bias and inclusion have moved the dialogue forward and are forms of advocacy. Curiosity and empathy develop

---

* Yassmin Abdel-Magied, "What Does My Headscarf Mean to You?" TED talk, May 27, 2015; https://www.ted.com/talks/yassmin_abdel_magied_what_does_my_headscarf_mean_to_you.

out of stories—stories that help people not just understand a statistic, but feel its impact. Personal stories of how real people have been affected by bias inspire others to consider the issue more fully and then to act.

Think of the last time you changed your mind on something important. What prompted you to change your mind? Was it a story, an experience, or a piece of data?

Here are some tips for sharing your story in a larger context:

- Browse viral social media posts for stories of bias that have entered the collective consciousness and sparked real change. What was their positive impact?

- Share your story on revealing and addressing bias through media that's appropriate for you. Make it a human story that helps people see you and understand your context and perspective.

MARK

My gayness is a part of my identity I kept hidden from everyone for many years. I had to come to terms with it myself first. Then I shared it with my family, my close friends, and eventually the people I worked with. As I've revealed, none of this was easy.

Sharing my story was an act of courage that started small—just my circle of family and closest friends—and steadily grew. I now share my story whenever I facilitate workshops on unconscious bias, and of course you've read about it in this book. Stories that don't see the light of day are never visible to others. A colleague might think nothing of asking a co-worker about their personal life. But if that person is worried that their sexual orientation or gender identity might be controversial, that simple question can be terrifying. In sharing my story, I hope I have shone a light on how challenging this might be. In spotlighting such challenges, we can generate change. For example, an invite to the company picnic might mention partners instead of spouses, and the company health-care plan might cover domestic partnerships instead of just traditional marriages.

Start where you're comfortable. As your courage increases, look for opportunities to expand your influence, not just for your sake, but for that of all those who can learn from or see themselves in your story.

Strategy: Speak Up

If you feel safe and supported in doing so, sometimes the best way to demonstrate courage is to identify the problem. Speaking up can be circumstantial and spontaneous, such as in a meeting or a conversation around the water cooler, or it can be bigger and bolder, like meeting formally with a senior leader to discuss an issue and possible solutions.

For example, in a recent mandatory training program for elected officials, we focused on making it safe for subordinates to speak up clearly and often. Having senior leaders sincerely state to the entire office or organization that they'd like issues brought to their attention, even if the issues are about them and there would be no professional penalty for raising such issues, can have a huge impact. By clearly communicating the desire to receive feedback and reassuring employees there will be no retaliation for doing so, senior leaders are empowering their employees to advocate for others and to provide important and necessary feedback benefiting the whole company.

Think of a time when you stood up for a belief or identified a problem. What made it easy or hard? What sort of response did you get?

Here are some tips for speaking up in a larger context:

- When you see bias happening to you or others, take a step back and look for evidence. Is this a trend, or something you've seen just once?

- Practice what you'd like to say. Practicing helps us move from the emotional part of the brain to the thinking part of the brain, where we can connect logically with others.

- Consider pulling the appropriate person aside and having this conversation in private.

- Use softening statements to begin the conversation.

Strategy: Formalize Dissent

Your organizational culture might not typically allow for disagreement. But when people are assigned the role of active dissenter, individuals can be rewarded or at least acknowledged for finding the flaws in an argument and pushing the group to think differently about problems and challenges.

Formalize the role of devil's advocate. When it comes to big decisions, having an individual in this role is essential to gain new perspectives. Whether you're looking to develop a new product or process or make an important strategic decision or plan, ask someone on your team to play the role of active dissenter or devil's advocate.

The devil's advocate should:

- Find the holes or gaps in a plan.

- Use empathy to consider fresh perspectives on the topic.

- Push back on any assumptions.

- Ensure that the role is about adding value and not just dissent for the sake of dissent. Poking holes in established norms is helpful; arguing about *everything* is not.

Strategy: Organize Networks

One of our primal needs is to form groups—us versus them. The powerful sense of groups can also accelerate performance. Research has shown that building networks to bring similar groups together can help counter the impact of bias on professional growth. They also formally connect marginalized groups to the informal networks proven to progress careers.

Historically, organizations have used the term "employee-resource group" for such networks, but most organizations far along the path of diversity and inclusion now also talk about affinity groups and business-resource groups. They each have different functions:

Employee-resource groups (ERGs) are about moving diverse candidates up through the pipeline of the organization and ensuring their access to opportunities. Such groups focus on coaching, mentoring, and sponsorship—activities that can boost the representation of targeted groups in management up to 24 percent.

As discussed, research consistently shows that when marginalized people advocate for their group, it can hurt them professionally over the long term. So one of the best practices is to enlist an executive sponsor who is not a member of the group. ERGs commonly focus on employees who share a unique perspective—as women, parents, veterans, people with a disability, or members of a specific race or religion or the LGBTQ+ community. ERGs can also exist around other identifiers or common interests. Effective ERGs provide educational opportunities, explore recruitment strategies to grow their community with top talent, and tie their goals to the strategic goals of their organization in a variety of ways.

Business-resource groups provide input to product development and cultural insights to the business. For example, Pepsi's African American business-resource group advises the organization on how to market new products to African American communities.

Affinity groups are very much like social clubs, offering employees the chance to go to happy hour together, engage in a group hobby like salsa dancing, build an informal group like a softball team, or just have fun outside of work.

When possible, offering all three types of groups allows people to participate according to their own objectives. I once worked on a team that administered an anonymous culture survey, and one of my colleagues wrote: "Because there are so many married people with children on the team, we don't do enough team building. We need kickball or happy hours." That's a valid suggestion, but with a grueling travel schedule, I was one of the team members who had no interest in after-hours activities. My colleague was looking for an affinity group, to bond with team members in a fun environment, whereas I was more interested in an ERG, to build relationships with executives and progress professionally. Having both types of groups available engages the whole team, whatever their interest.

Can people who are allies join resource groups? Across the board, anyone can join a resource group. People get involved in groups for different reasons, and joining as an ally can build tremendous empathy. One of my clients recently started several employee-resource groups, and at the kick-off meeting, the executive champion for the ERG for people with disabilities shared his story about his three sons on the autism spectrum. He cared very much about the role of people with disabilities in the workplace and the contribution they could make, which was why he was the executive champion for that group. Another executive sponsor told a story about the first time someone mentioned how different he looked from his daughter, whom he adopted from China, and why that mattered to him.

Here are some tips for thinking about organizing networks. Ask yourself:

- Do I feel left out of formal or informal networks at work?

- Are there experiences I have that I don't feel like my team can relate to?

- Are there networks at work or in my community that could help me feel understood and supported? If not, can I organize one?

ANNE

I believe that we at AT&T are world-class at employee-resource groups and employee networks. We have over two dozen of these groups, organized around many different constituents. I'm the executive sponsor of the AT&T Women of Business employee network and the Asian Pacific Women's Organization. We have groups focused on veterans, our native and indigenous employees, and many others.

It's important for any leader to support these communities and the gathering of constituent groups. If these organizations don't exist, enable them. If they already exist, join them.

One of the greatest misconceptions about women's organizations is that you have to be a woman to join one. This is not true! I know many men who say the best mentoring they've received has been through our women's networks. These networks broaden your perspective and your network beyond your normal day-to-day activities and routines.

Additionally, joining groups outside your experience can allow you to align yourself with them. Recently one of my male clients started a women's network. His role as the champion of that women's network is priceless, because that group of women—as well as the male allies—know that the CEO is committed to this.

If your organization lacks these types of networks, start them! You need only a couple of people. And with technology, you can create a global community. Be sure to enlist executive sponsors at the outset to increase the probability of success through visible support and championing.

Chapter 13: Courage to Be an Advocate
Reflection for Individuals

"Courage to Be an Advocate" Strategies

- Share Your Story

- Speak Up

- Formalize Dissent

- Organize Networks

Bias Scenario

You're a recruiter at a Fortune 500 company. Although you work hard to propose a diverse slate of candidates, you notice that one leader consistently rejects people with foreign- or diverse-sounding names.

1. What bias(es) might be in play?

....

....

....

....

2. How might those bias(es) impact your work or the company's (Performance Model)?

....

....

....

....

3. Which "Courage to Be an Advocate" strategy would you utilize in this situation, and why?

....

....

....

....

....

....

....

....

....

....

....

....

....

....

....

....

....

....

....

Chapter 13: Courage to Be an Advocate
Application for Leaders

Bias Scenario

You've recently accepted a leadership position at a new organization with a high-performing, highly engaged team. As you review the budget, you notice that the team members of equal experience and performance are being compensated very differently.

1. What bias(es) might be at play?

....

....

....

....

2. How might those bias(es) impact the team's work or your work (Performance Model)?

....

....

....

....

3. Which "Courage to Be an Advocate" strategy would you utilize in this situation, and why?

....

....

....

....

....

Additional Reflection

Now that you've reviewed eight scenarios and thought about how to apply all sixteen courage strategies, can you think of a real-life circumstance you are facing?

....

....

....

....

Outline the components of the circumstance. What bias(es) might be at play and how might the bias(es) impact your work and the work of those in the circumstance?

....

....

....

....

What courage strategy would you utilize in this situation and why?

....

....

....

....

You don't see diversity change in a month, in two months, in six months. You see it in a year, you see it in two years, in five years. That's how it works. It's a long game, and very few companies are in it for the long game. . . . Leaders have to communicate "I'm in it for the long game, and I won't stop looking at this." *

—Bo Young Lee, chief of diversity and inclusion, Uber

* Barbara Booth, "How Troubled Ride-Hailing Giant Uber Put an End to Internal 'Name-Calling and Finger-Pointing,'" CNBC, November 29, 2018; https://www.cnbc.com/2018/11/29/how-uber-put-an-end-to-internal-name-calling-and-finger-pointing-.html.

Part 4: Apply Across the Talent Lifecycle

ANNE

As leaders and managers, we must realize that unconscious bias is resident in each one of us and also present within the embedded governance, systems of decision making, and processes across our organizations. This is perhaps most prevalent throughout the key phases of the Talent Lifecycle, and if we don't address it proactively, this bias will remain and serve as an inhibitor to the development of high-performing teams who deliver world-class results.

One of the most vital aspects of creating and building strong teams is the creation of a robust pipeline of talent in the organization. From a Talent Lifecycle standpoint, you can think of this as the marketing, recruiting, and staffing processes required to ensure that the best people—those who can bring the will and skills you need—are attracted to your brand and have an interest in working with you. Does bias exist in your current approach? Is the way you recruit including the where and how dated? Are you winning the talent battles in your industry? Do you feel that your pipeline is reflective not only of the talent you need now, but of the talent you need for the future?

Once someone has decided to join your team, how are you developing them? What's your approach to training, learning, and support? How does your organization approach mentorship? Are you focused on the whole person, or just the work persona? How engaged are your employees? How do you identify high-potential talent? And are those approaches dated? Does that high-potential talent represent the diverse set of leaders you know you need both now and later? I'd venture to say that there's likely bias embedded in the answers to these questions—and that it's worth exploring if you want your organizational culture to evolve at the pace of the market and stay ahead of existing and emerging competitors.

And how about career advancement? What does that high-potential list of employees look like? Is it more homogenous than diverse? Are you struggling to build a bench of succession, or do your candidates tend to come from the same place in your organization? Is there an archetype of a leader who is successful in your company? And is it reflective of the market you're competing in today—and will that bench best prepare you for the competition of the future? How are talent roundtables facilitated today? Does everyone have an equal voice, or are some voices at the table more dominant than others? Should they be?

I'm not asking all of these rhetorical questions to frustrate you. Rather, I'm using them in a way to help bring to the surface the possibility and notion of bias built into your decision-making systems and structures. The vitality of your workforce is key to its success. If your organization does not take a purposeful look and a periodic relook at how it supports and manages its talent, biases can reign, thus inadvertently holding the organization back from the progress, innovation, and transformation you require.

I recently worked with a client, a healthcare technology company, on their diversity and inclusion strategy. The strategy session was particularly focused on two things: the Talent Lifecycle, and initiating a diversity and inclusion council. Before the session, I'd had several planning calls with the leader responsible for learning and development, a real champion of inclusion at this organization. She was eager to make some progress and ensure a sound strategy around D&I for the company. One thing stood out to me in these planning calls and even in our session: this leader kept reiterating that the strategy couldn't be about quotas. I asked her to tell me more about this, and she shared that, years ago, a consultant had been brought in to help build a D&I strategy. The consultant gave a briefing on her recommendations to the executive team, and her thesis was that the firm needed to set quotas around racial groups and gender and work aggressively to meet those quotas. The executive team did not react well.

This speaks to the evolution of the D&I professional and this space. When leaders are asked about diversity and inclusion and the Talent Lifecycle, many of them default to affirmative action and quotas. If they are in the majority, this often triggers the primitive part of their brain. "Are you saying you need to replace me to fill this quota?" These feelings of scarcity can result in very limiting, even damaging treatment of employees who may be seen as the "diversity hire."

Another challenge I've seen with quotas is that they often become the ceiling instead of the floor. This can lead to tokenism—the idea that a firm made a "diversity hire" to meet a quota, not because the person was the most qualified and capable for the role. "See, we have a woman, a Black person, a veteran" and so forth. Imagine how limiting it would feel if someone referred to you as the "diversity hire," thus negating the great deal of time and energy you've put into your education and career.

Most countries outside the United States are not even allowed to collect demographic data on their employees. Even in the United States, this data is used as a benchmark, not a firm goal. While hiring quotas have largely been eliminated, this sense of tokenism remains as leaders consider diversity-hiring initiatives and has given way to "two-kenism"—the idea that if we have at least two people in a particular group represented, we've met our goals. This mindset and approach can be limiting.

Instead, our discussion of the Talent Lifecycle is focused on how we can genuinely and sincerely apply the principles of self-awareness, openness, and growth to the Talent Lifecycle—not because we're obligated to do so, but because we recognize that diversity and inclusion are critical to sustain a high-performing organization. By implementing the tactics outlined in Part 4, leaders can ensure that leadership behavior, people-related processes, and organizational culture reinforce the High-Performance Zone, where employees feel valued, respected, and included.

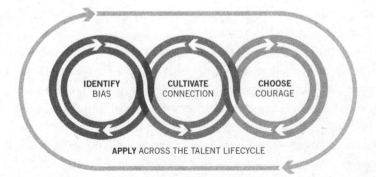

Frame/Reframe

Frame:	Reframe:
The Talent Lifecycle is mandated HR law and policy. As a leader, I just follow the policy.	The Talent Lifecycle is guided by HR law and policy. As a leader, I can influence and impact the experience of employees at every point in the lifecycle.

The Principle of Purpose

We've made the case for introspection, vulnerability, empathy, curiosity, and courage to build high-performing teams. But you need to agree. As a leader, you need to see diversity and inclusion as a critical component of your leadership purpose and approach. If you agree, then what follows is a road map for applying that purpose across the Talent Lifecycle. The Talent Lifecycle consists of the processes and decisions in your team and organization that impact people. As is true of most of the best things in life, treating diversity and inclusion as a priority is easier said than done but not impossible. It'll take courage to apply what you've learned, to look back at your responses to the tools thus far and do something different. But such actions will align with your larger leadership purpose, and you will see the positive results in your performance and the performance of your teams.

The Talent Lifecycle encompasses the decision points that occur across someone's career: if they are hired, what projects they are assigned to, and whether they get promoted or not. There are innumerable variations of the Talent Lifecycle, as this model varies slightly across industries and organizations. For example, I worked with a consulting firm whose Talent Lifecycle included internal project assignments because of the way their consultants were assigned to client sites. So there were essentially two levels of selection: the first, employment with the firm; the second, incorporation into a client team. For our purposes, we'll classify the decisions of the Talent Lifecycle under three categories: Getting Hired, Contributing and Engaging, and Moving Up.

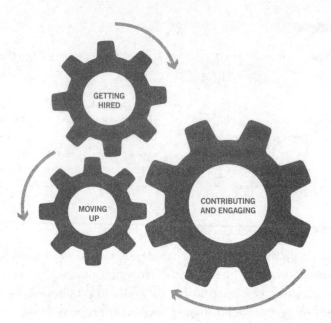

We usually see the Talent Lifecycle as one continuous cycle. For example, we are hired by an organization, work there for a few years, get a promotion, then leave the organization and begin again at a new organization through a lateral or upward move. For our purposes, I'd like you to think of these three categories as more interdependent. These are gears that turn one another. The employee benefits, deemed as important at one point in a career, might change over time. The development opportunities available at any given organization will impact employee engagement and the reputation of the organization in the marketplace, which ultimately impact what the applicant pool looks like. Each component of the Talent Lifecycle and the decisions, policies, procedures, and norms in that component are intrinsically connected to the others.

Granted, this is *a lot* to consider! The idea here is not that you would transform your organization's entire Talent Lifecycle. Instead, we want to ensure that as a leader, you attempt to understand each component of the Talent Lifecycle and the decisions that happen in each part of the model, then think about where you might optimize. When it comes to applying bias-mitigation strategies to the Talent Lifecycle, I'm often asked, "Which component should we start with?" Organizations wonder if they should focus on broadening recruitment and hiring, diversifying their board, or building a women's leadership-pipeline program, for example.

Which component you begin with depends on what the Talent Lifecycle looks like in your organization. What are your organization's strengths and opportunities? What does your current quantitative and qualitative data say about where the performance gaps are? Do you even *have* such data? And if not, how can you get it?

Let's say your organization is at the vanguard of diversity-recruiting programs and has implemented blind résumé reviews (all identity data such as name and gender has been removed), panel interviews, and joint hiring decisions. But your employee-engagement data is low, especially for veterans, people of color, and women. You might have real trouble retaining new hires beyond two years and decide to start there. Conversely, you'd start in a different place if you have a family-owned business that's fairly homogenous and maintains high employee engagement, retention, and incredible customer loyalty—but faces significant growth.

Both scenarios give you a sense of where to point your efforts. In the first circumstance, you'd start with employee experience and the components of Contributing and Engaging. In the second, you might focus specifically on Getting Hired recruitment processes in light of the significant growth you are facing. Whatever your reality, the first step is understanding your current state and where bias may be impacting performance the most in your specific Talent Lifecycle.

ANNE

A decision many encounter in their careers is whether or not to move from the role of an individual contributor to one with direct supervisory responsibilities. Many assume this is a straightforward transition and that everyone aspires to manage people. Nothing could be further from the truth. I encourage those who are interested in a career path that involves the direct leadership of the team to first seek leadership opportunities through projects, special assignments, and even situational environments like meetings or group conversations. To develop and assert one's leadership takes practice and experiences. And as we all know, leaders are all about people—inspiring them, coaching them, developing them and, yes, leading them. Leadership is not a static practice.

Ultimately, every leader must understand, shape, and support the full Talent Lifecycle—for their people, teams, and organization as a whole. A key objective of leadership is to ensure that you have the right team on the field at the right time . . . which includes having the right people in the right roles at that point. With the pace of change accelerating and the marketplace dynamically evolving, leaders must ensure they are constantly calibrating and recalibrating whether their organization is poised for success not just in the present, but into the future.

Finally, while there is a full complement of legality that accompanies any manner of human resources decision and procedure, I find that organizations often suffer from a lack of imagination. In this part, we've scratched the surface of best practices and questions to consider as you look at the Talent Lifecycle. As you implement improvements, this is an opportunity to color outside the lines. The term "intersectionality" didn't exist until attorney and advocate Kimberlé Williams Crenshaw coined it in her defense of a civil-rights case.* Now intersectionality, the notion that there is interconnectedness in our social categorizations and identifiers like race, class, sexual orientation, and gender identity defines diversity and inclusion initiatives globally. The concept of amplification didn't exist until a group of senior women in the Obama White House conceived and implemented it. Now, amplification is used broadly to recognize the contribution of traditionally marginalized women across organizations. Google's large-scale study of what makes great teams led to simple but profound strategies like a psychological safety checklist for managers. And creating agile teams is an idea that works only because organizations are willing to reject traditional command-and-control hierarchies. The Bill and Melinda Gates Foundation offers fifty-two weeks of paid parental leave. Marc Benioff,

---

* Kimberlé Crenshaw, "Demarginalizing the Intersection of Race and Sex: A Black Feminist Critique of Antidiscrimination Doctrine, Feminist Theory, and Antiracist Politics." *University of Chicago Legal Forum,* vol. 1989, article 8; https://chicagoun bound.uchicago.edu/uclf/vol1989/iss1/8.

CEO of Salesforce, dedicated $6 million over two years to correcting the pay gap by gender, race, and ethnicity across the company.

Granted, some of these strategies require a budget; the financial reality each organization faces might not allow for such broad, sweeping decisions. But many inclusive leadership behaviors and strategies have little to no cost. We are bound only by our imagination and by what we don't allow ourselves to do. As a leader at any level, you have influence and can make an impact that enhances possibilities across the organization.

Chapter 14: Getting Hired

I cannot tell you how many times I had a rock-star phone interview because obviously. *But when I got there, I literally had one man walk in, look me up and down, and walk out. . . . That dude lost out on an awesome employee, so that damaged him. His own fat phobia damaged him.*

You're going to limit your talent pool if you allow us to be pushed out. Because some of us, I'd say most of us, like any other group of people, we're awesome. You should use us. We're great people. Just because I need to take the elevator and not the stairs every day does not make me less of an employee. It doesn't make me less seen. It doesn't make me less useful to an organization.

—Lisa Love, coordinating producer, PBS's Emmy Award–winning
    *SciGirls**

Getting Hired consists of the decisions that determine whether someone has a seat at the table: *recruitment, hiring and interviewing, and employee benefits.* It includes questions like how a position is advertised, what information is included in the job description, how interviews are conducted and by whom, what the interviewing process consists of, and how the final hiring decision is made.

Compensation is also a part of Getting Hired: how salaries are determined, what benefits are offered to whom, and how the negotiation

---

* Love, Lisa. "What is the Big Fat Deal?" Presentation. Forum for Workplace Inclusion, 2018.

GETTING HIRED

RECRUITMENT

Examine Your Opportunity for Partnerships

Consider the Future of Work

Use Data, Not Just Instincts, for Hiring Criteria

Optimize Your Job Descriptions

HIRING AND INTERVIEWING

Create Trained Hiring Panels

Allow Complements to the Résumé

Align the Interview to the Job

EMPLOYEE BENEFITS

Conduct an Inclusion Audit of Your Benefits Programs

Ensure a Pay Audit Is Included

Allow for Flexibility and Negotiation

Believe the Data

Signal Everyone

Check Yourself

process is carried out. You might consider employee benefits an issue for once you are hired in an organization, but benefits can also determine whether certain applicants even consider applying, interviewing, and/or accepting a position in the organization. The seemingly simple decision of whether internships are paid or unpaid can significantly skew the applicant pool, for example. Benefits such as parental leave, health insurance, flexible work arrangements, and formal development opportunities are all important considerations for many candidates. Whether an organization supports work visas could determine if they are a viable option for international talent. It's also important to assess relocation policies and the way organizations do or do not support life transitions like accommodating caretaking, providing on-ramps and off-ramps for those who need to temporarily leave and reenter the workforce for whatever reason, supporting disability, and allowing for sabbaticals. Sometimes these policies disproportionately impact some demographic groups over others.

Recruitment

Many managers assume hiring is HR's job, but if they're committed to diversifying the workforce to improve results, they'll need to take a more active role. Bias, as we've established, impacts our decision making. And recruitment and hiring are some of the most critical decisions we make about people's careers.

Recruitment focuses on how a position is advertised, who gets to know about the position, and how the information is distributed. One common challenge we've heard from clients (which the research confirms) is the limited pools from which recruitment draws. For example, if you rely on current employees to refer candidates or advertise only at specific universities or websites, you're recruiting only within limited networks. If you've had the same recruitment strategy for an extended period of time, you haven't widened and diversified your applicant pool. You can cast the net wider with these four strategies.

Examine Your Opportunity for Partnerships

One of the most common pushbacks around hiring is when leaders argue their hands are tied because they simply don't receive applications from many qualified diverse candidates. Additionally, discussing many identifiers—sexual orientation, marital status, age, race—is off the table during the hiring process. Leaders will say, "How am I supposed to hire more gay employees? I can't ask people if they're gay, right? How do I get more diversity if I can't ask those questions?" Partnerships are a relatively easy and accessible way to broaden your applicant pool without asking invasive questions during the hiring process.

Partnering with historically Black colleges and universities is a common best practice, but it's less commonly used to recruit people from other underrepresented groups. You can reach out to academic institutions to market to their first-generation and veteran students, their LGBTQ+ organizations, or their office of disability services. Consider instituting internships and co-op programs, where people work and go to school, to further diversify your applicant pool.

Not looking for entry-level candidates? Partnerships can also be formed with alumni organizations, fraternal organizations, the Department of Veterans Affairs or other veteran-serving institutions, international embassies, and advocacy groups for various populations to include religion, sexual orientation, gender identity, race, and gender.

Some programs intended to help with recruitment can unintentionally hinder the diversity of your candidates, such as employee referral programs. If it's not part of a larger recruitment strategy, recruiting through existing employees' networks may perpetuate the existing applicant pool. If you do have a referral program, work with your employee-resource groups to ensure those referral programs are extending widely enough.

Consider the Future of Work

Some organizations struggle with the recruitment of diverse or younger candidates because they're still fixated on traditional models of employment. I've heard horror stories about applicants inquiring about telework and being dropped from consideration. But why? The future of work is, for better or worse, built around the gig economy. Digital nomads are looking for project-based work and flexibility. Even those looking for full-time work and the ability to grow within an organization are prioritizing the ability to live and work anywhere while making a contribution. Expand your view of what work will look like in the future and ensure you're recruiting with that in mind.

Some companies without diverse workforces say their population simply reflects the population of their location. But new models of work can allow you to circumvent that issue. The Defense Logistics Agency (DLA) is a federal agency that provides the U.S. military with the equipment and services it needs to carry out its critical functions. A few years ago, they decided to remove geographic location from their job announcements. You can live anywhere and apply for any job with DLA. They made that decision intentionally to broaden their applicant pool—and it worked.

Consider the possibility that positions in your organization could be done off-site, and think about opening them up to applicants outside your geographic area. Perhaps you could contract out work and use a contract as an on-ramp to the organization.

Use Data, Not Just Instincts, for Hiring Criteria

A client of mine, a former recruiter, told me about a manager who had an opening on his team. This manager insisted that any new hire have a specific degree from a specific school. The recruiter said, "Is there a reason behind that?" The manager couldn't articulate why, beyond a general sense of prestige.

To his credit, the recruiter pushed the manager and said, "Why don't we hold off on that school for a moment and zoom out. What is the role you need to fill, and what competencies are you looking for? What attitudes are you looking for? What's working on your current team?"

The recruiter then analyzed the résumés of the existing team and found that none of them had that special degree or had gone to that type of school. The recruiter returned to the manager with the data and said, "This is the profile of your current team, which you're happy with, and this is what you say you're looking for. So instead of recruiting at this specific school for this specific degree, why don't we put together a position description that better reflects the competencies you're look- ing for?" They were able to recruit a talented team member they would have excluded if they'd kept the original requirements.

That manager had an idea in his head (*this school is good; other schools aren't*) and registered only information that confirmed it—con- firmation bias in action. His vague impression of the prestige the spe- cific degree would bring was a shortcut and wasn't based on the actual facts of high-performance competencies on his team. Because the re- cruiter dug deeper to figure out the facts, he was able to broaden the applicant pool in the process.

What does your applicant pool look like? What does success on your team look like? Conduct entry interviews to better understand where candidates are learning about the job and what interested them about it—then document the data instead of letting confirmation bias bolster your preconceptions.

Optimize Your Job Descriptions

Many organizations use legacy descriptions year after year. The job description hasn't changed in a decade, but the job has. Update your job descriptions regularly to properly communicate the required competencies.

While you're at it, make sure you aren't limiting your applicant pool with overly narrow requirements about past experience.

Talent experts Josh Bersin and Tomas Chamorro-Premuzic explain: "If you move beyond promoting those with the most competence and start thinking more about those who can get you where you want to go, your company will thrive."*

As you consider job descriptions, add an additional filtering question to the requirements: *Is this credential a requirement of the role, or something we assume is required based on the status of the job?*

Military service, for example, is very difficult to translate to a private-sector job description. Look at the way private-sector job descriptions are written—rarely will they list a requirement like "ten to fifteen years of senior management experience or the military equivalent." These are the same organizations who want more veterans working for them, but they're not allowing for translation.

Finally, consider the language in the job description. Avoid gendered terms like "rockstar" and "ninja," sports language like "tackle" and "heavy hitter," and jargon or acronyms with no meaning outside of your organization. This language can be unintentionally limiting for applicants. Most organizations include an EEOC compliance statement affirming they are an equal opportunity employer and do not discriminate.

---

* Josh Bersin and Tomas Chamorro-Premuzic, "Hire Leaders for What They Can Do, Not What They Have Done." *Harvard Business Review*, August 27, 2019; https://hbr.org/2019/08/hire-leaders-for-what-they-can-do-not-what-they-have-done.

Two-thirds of job seekers are evaluating a company on their diversity,* so be up-front about your priorities in the job description. Go beyond compliance by including your organization's values and commitment to diversity, equity, and inclusion; be sure to say why these matter to your organization.

ANNE

Many underestimate the criticality of their hiring pipeline. The vitality of any workforce is key to its success—and in order to have vitality, you must be constantly focused on the incoming pipeline. I've seen organizations make the mistake of shutting off that pipeline and hunkering down on their existing employee base. I've also seen organizations focus only on their external recruiting efforts without focus on developing their existing employee base. Here's the issue with a binary approach: Times change. Technology changes. The market changes. Customer preferences change. Your competitors change. You may believe that your competitive differentiators are your products or services or pricing or experience. Bottom line: none of that is possible without the right people who are empowered by the right culture. Your competitive advantage is your people. And there's no question that just as the marketplace is ultracompetitive across every sector for customers, it is even more so for talent. We all want the best people on our team, and this requires that we focus on ensuring that the talent we have is the talent we need.

Leaders must ensure that their HR processes are aligned with their vision for their workforce. This includes not just where and how you recruit, but why. The value proposition you develop for your prospective employees is just as important as that which you develop for your customers. They are intertwined.

As we know, unconscious bias can really hurt us in our ability to attract

---

* "Two Thirds of People Consider Diversity Important When Deciding Where to Work, Glassdoor Survey." Glassdoor, November 17, 2014; https://www.glassdoor.com/about-us/twothirds-people-diversity-important-deciding-work-glassdoor-survey-2/.

and recruit the best talent. The best talent of yesterday and today may not be the best talent for the future. How often have we heard that adage "Hire for will, not for skill"? Well, I'd argue that you need to hire for both, but we must think more broadly and strategically about skill. In the past, skills represented hardened knowledge, without much value placed on human skills. We must require all of it—will, hard and soft skills, and behaviors. The more diverse our talent is, the better and more innovative our results will be. And as such, you've got to ensure that your leadership and HR practices are as contemporary as you desire your workforce to be.

Of course, this doesn't happen overnight, and it requires internal and external investment—consistent over time—to be successful. Think of it as an investment in your brand. Just as you need your brand to speak to your customers and represent who you are as a company, you need your brand to do the same for those who will represent your future workforce. And your hiring brand will be shaped by your presence in the market and on campuses, your benefits, feedback from others who have worked for you or interviewed with you, and more.

MARK

In my experience with clients, organizations who say they value inclusion but *don't* do the hard work of living that value create much more cynicism and skepticism than engagement.

On the other hand, organizations who are very clear about how they value inclusion and how that is reflected across the Talent Lifecycle and employee experience are vastly more successful. Ultimately, inclusion lives not only as a beautiful statement in the annual report or on the website, but in the behaviors and actions of the organization's people at every level. As Dr. Covey used to say, "You can't talk yourself out of a problem you behaved yourself into."

As you consider your recruitment practices and all the steps of the Talent Lifecycle, ask yourself, "Is inclusion reflected in how we do this?"

Hiring and Interviewing

Unfortunately, much of the hiring process has nothing to do with actual performance. In Dolly Chugh's book *The Person You Mean to Be*, she cites research at a big consulting firm that revealed a majority of the job-interview time was actually spent talking about elite hobbies and schools.[*] More golf, rowing, and the Ivy League—less metrics, job functions, and skills. Hiring decisions were based on these points of conversation, as opposed to the person's ability to do the job—a process that would have an obvious effect on the equity of opportunity for diverse candidates.

The hiring process can be very subjective. Data shows that if I'm left-handed, I'll feel more fondness for a candidate sitting to the left of me than one sitting to the right of me.[†] And I might feel warmth for a candidate who opts for a warm drink, and chilled by a candidate who asks for a cold drink. It's important for us to draw from what we've already said about self-awareness. The baseline for good recruitment is being aware of the feelings stirred up as you interact with different candidates. If you encounter negative feelings, be sure to check them against possible biases. Here are some strategies for mitigating negative bias in the hiring and selection process.

Create Trained Hiring Panels

Move away from 1-on-1 interviews. We know that many of our instincts and decisions are guided by bias. With that in mind, collaborate across perspectives to mitigate bias. Build a process whereby hiring officials are required to complete training on bias, effective interviewing skills, and determining competency and skill. Require that *multiple* hiring officials participate in and collaborate during interviews. Depending on the size and scope of your organization, that number might vary. For many organizations, panels consist of three individuals: the hiring manager or

---

[*] Dolly Chugh, *The Person You Mean to Be: How Good People Fight Bias.* New York: Harper Business, 2018.

[†] Christine Blackman, "Lefty or Righty? A New Hold on How We Think." *Stanford News,* August 4, 2009; https://news.stanford.edu/news/2009/august3/lefty-deci sion-study-080509.html.

person the role will report to, a peer manager the role might collaborate with, and a next-level boss or colleague to the role. Sometimes they also include a subordinate, which can be a powerful statement that every voice matters in leadership decisions. Complete the process by debriefing interviews immediately following the session so that the experience isn't skewed by time. The greater the amount of time between the interview and the debriefing, the more we lean into how the interview made us feel instead of what actually happened.

MARK

When I first started with Franklin International Institute in 1992, the final step in the hiring process consisted of a two-part panel interview with several people from various areas within the company. The panel members weren't just from L&D (Learning and Development), but also from a wide range of areas such as operations, sales, the warehouse, finance, and so forth.

I was given all of the facilitator materials and the preparation time needed to facilitate one of the current workshops at the time. When I felt ready, I was flown to the corporate office, where I facilitated a half hour of their choosing to the group. I then answered questions from the various panel members about any aspect of the entire course they felt an actual participant might have.

Afterward, the panel met and shared with one another their feedback. The group then came to consensus on a hiring decision. I felt more comfortable with a panel interview than I would have felt talking to a single interviewer. There was comfort in knowing my future wasn't in the hands of just one person. It also gave me greater insight into multiple aspects of the organization. In a sense, it gave me the ability to "interview" them. I was able to experience a bit of the organizational culture in a microcosm. The decision wasn't made by one person and a single piece of paper. Panel interviews can offer greater perspective and less bias, and provide an opportunity to see how well the candidate fits in with the organization's culture and whether the candidate has the skills required for the job. It also provides the candidate with some of those same insights.

Allow Complements to the Résumé

Résumés can be limiting. Instead of being a true reflection of a person's experience, they often indicate someone's writing ability or ability to pay for a professional résumé writer. While the résumé provides a factual baseline concerning a person's prior experience and education, there are alternatives or supplemental application components that can better highlight a person's talent, capabilities, and possibilities.

For technical positions like coding, more and more organizations are asking applicants to complete sample projects instead of simply submitting a résumé. We can extend that practice to many nontechnical job functions as well. One of my clients asks their consulting applicants to come to the interview prepared to give a presentation and deliver a live facilitation of their content. Another organization asks potential project managers to outline how they would approach a project scenario. Submission of prior work can serve the same function of going beyond the standard résumé. Design portfolios, writing clips, and video reels are already common in their respective fields, but get creative in how this component could apply to other job functions.

Product-based interviewing is another strategy to level the playing field. Candidates might not have a prestigious degree or a blue-chip résumé, but they have an opportunity to show you their potential through the only thing that matters—their work.

Align the Interview to the Job

The word "interview" likely conjures a similar image for you as it does for me: Wear a suit; show up to an office at an appointed day and time, copies of your résumé clutched in your hand; wait in the reception area to be escorted into an office or a conference room for an interview; then answer questions about your background, what you know about the job, why you want it, and how you might approach it. For those of us who work in a traditional office, this interview might be the right format. But if the job is not a traditional one, think about how you can better align the interview to the role. This could mean an outdoor walking interview for a groundskeeper or a classroom-based interview for an educator. Putting the candidate in the environment of their role ensures they can perform at their best and shows you how they might actually perform in the role.

Employee Benefits

Conduct an Inclusion Audit of Your Benefits Programs

Several organizations will perform an inclusion audit on your employee benefits. We've certainly seen an evolution in these policies over the last decade to include things like the transition from "maternity leave" to "parental leave" to "bonding leave." In this case, the language literally opens the benefit up to more individuals and circumstances. Many organizations have also implemented longer bonding leave and paid leave over and above what is required by law. The same is true of health coverage and who it applies to—spouse or domestic partner. Benefits also include formal things like access to appropriate and comfortable facilities for nursing and pumping, quantity of paid time off, flexible work schedules, and work-from-home policies. I've seen companies flex their holiday schedules to be more inclusive of a broad range of holidays celebrated by various religions and cultures. They also include more informal benefits like health and wellness programs, social responsibility or other giveback programs. From the perspective of a profit-and-loss (P&L) statement, the impetus might be to find ways to keep the cost of benefits down each year. But I would recommend doing an inclusion audit to learn what gaps might exist and how those gaps might be impacting recruitment and retention, which also impact the P&L.

Ensure a Pay Audit Is Included

Perhaps the most prominent employee benefit is compensation. Many people with expertise greater than my own have researched and written about the gender and racial pay gaps. For the purposes of examining the Talent Lifecycle at your organization, I'd recommend including a pay audit in your larger inclusion audit of employee benefits. In my experience, organizations scoff when a gender or racial pay gap is mentioned. Leadership might insist that people are compensated based on their experience, title, and results. They might also dismiss the conversation altogether, citing privacy and confidentiality. But the only way to truly know if there is a disparity is to review the data. FranklinCovey routinely performs pay audits to ensure equal pay for equal work.

Allow for Flexibility and Negotiation

In 2018, global staffing firm Robert Half in Menlo Park, California, found that 68 percent of men and 45 percent of women negotiated their salaries. The fact that women are less likely to ask for more money has been written about a lot. But I think the story is more complex than that. Research published in January 2019 found that when given the chance, women are as likely as men to negotiate their salary—but that opportunity simply doesn't present itself as often for women. The Australian researchers in this case found that a significantly higher proportion of men in their sample indicated they have the opportunity to negotiate pay (49 percent of men and 35 percent of women respectively). This shows that the issue is not necessarily that women don't ask; instead, it's that they are less likely to be signaled that negotiation is feasible.*

When looking at raises once someone is in a position, researchers found in 2018 that women ask for raises as often as men but are less likely to get them, leading one to surmise that the bar might be higher for women.† In conversations about the gender pay gap or pay gaps that exist around other dimensions with leaders, I've been asked, "Is it my responsibility to teach someone how to negotiate? It's not my fault they're not advocating for themselves." I understand this perspective, but if our goal is high performance and the mitigation of bias in the Talent Lifecycle, perhaps we are more responsible than we'd previously imagined. How can we even the playing field in terms of negotiation and compensation?

Believe the Data

There might be an instinct to explain away pay discrepancies in compensation—for example, by saying the work between two individuals isn't exactly the same or one person has been here two years longer

---

* Kathy Gurchiek, "Study: Women Negotiate Pay When Given the Chance." SHRM, May 20, 2019; https://www.shrm.org/hr-today/news/hr-news/pages/more-pro fessionals-are-negotiating-salaries-than-in-the-past.aspx.

† Benjamin Artz, Amanda Goodall, and Andrew J. Oswald, "Research: Women Ask for Raises as Often as Men, but Are Less Likely to Get Them." *Harvard Business Review,* June 25, 2018; https://hbr.org/2018/06/research-women-ask-for-raises -as-often-as-men-but-are-less-likely-to-get-them.

than another, so this has nothing to do with the second person's disability. Perceived status based on credentials or background could come into play or ableist language dismissing someone based on their disability or even stereotypes around who is easier to work with or more agreeable. So if the compensation audit says there is a pay gap, if promotion data says it takes longer for one group to progress than another, or if entry and exit interviews show a discrepancy in how negotiations are handled, take this information at face value. There's something to it.

Signal Everyone

You can do some simple things to signal that negotiation is possible. When you provide a written offer, give candidates at least twenty-four hours to respond. Let them know you are available for any questions or concerns they might have. If a candidate does come back with a counteroffer, give them an opportunity to make their case. Why do they believe a higher offer is warranted or necessary? Then think creatively about what is available. Perhaps you don't have the budget to meet the salary requirement, but other employee benefits may be on the table. Be open to the possibilities

Check Yourself

The hiring-panel strategy works for salary negotiations as well. Bring in HR, peers, and research from platforms like Glassdoor so your response to a request for a salary increase is not simply a visceral reaction, but a response accurately based on capabilities, market rates, and organizational standards.

Chapter 14: Getting Hired
Reflection for Individuals

The tools in this chapter and the next two chapters are going to walk you through an audit of your Talent Lifecycle. If you are not a human resources professional, think outside of the boundaries of your normal engagement with this lifecycle. Then engage members of your team and leadership to consider implementing change.

1. Reflect on your experiences around recruitment, hiring, or benefits. Have you personally experienced (or seen other examples) where such decisions were likely made through the lens of bias? If so, what was the impact to you and others involved?

   ....

   ....

   ....

2. How does operating through a lens of performance mitigate possible entry biases?

   ....

   ....

   ....

3. How might recruitment, hiring, or benefit distribution applied through the lens of bias decrease morale, discretionary effort, and retention?

   ....

   ....

   ....

Chapter 14: Getting Hired
Application for Leaders

Consider your culture and practices when it comes to recruitment, hiring, and benefit distribution for your team.

1. List the possible biases that might be in play.

....

....

....

....

2. How could an increase in empathy and curiosity add new insight into the costs of such practices?

....

....

....

....

3. Where might you apply careful or bold courage to make a change?

....

....

....

....

....

....

Chapter 15: Contributing and Engaging

*An inclusive onboarding experience is like adding someone to your game of musical chairs: You can't add someone new without stopping the music and adding a chair. Creating a meaningful experience means slowing down, making adjustments, and including your new hire.**

—Sonja Gittens-Ottley, head of diversity and inclusion, Asana

Contributing and Engaging is focused on the period after you're hired at the organization and includes onboarding, engagement, and retention strategies. What is the process for onboarding, and is it consistent across career fields, locations, and people? Are there mentoring and coaching opportunities? How are assignments given and teams formed? What sorts of networks exist in the organization? And does the organization look at employee engagement and retention data, then deploy proactive strategies to improve that data?

MARK

While I was working with a group of high-potential leaders at a federal agency, the subject of organizational "fit" came up. We had been discussing some of the places where unconscious bias can be experienced throughout the Talent Lifecycle—specifically, some of the potential dangers of focusing on organizational "fit" as we looked at hiring, but also

---

* Sonja Gittens-Ottley, "Inclusion Starts on Day One: 10 Ways to Build an Inclusive Onboarding Experience." Asana Wavelength; https://wavelength.asana.com/inclusive-onboarding-experience/.

promotions, work assignments, and team dynamics. "Fit" is a very small word with very large implications.

Someone asked, "What's wrong with a focus on fit? Isn't it important that our employees fit with the organization's values?" A very good question. We're often more receptive to ideas we've come to on our own instead of having been told what the right answer is. "Fit" is a word with a lot of emotional weight for some people, who feel strongly that their gut instinct on fit is how you make a good decision. An interesting conversation ensued. This is where we ultimately landed.

When "fit" means the person's values and beliefs are in line with the organization's culture, core values, and mission, there is a greater chance of success. But there are potential red flags if "fit" is being used to describe how characteristics lend themselves to in-group bias or if "fit" is ensuring someone won't make waves or be disruptive—the word we settled on was "agreeable." Cultural fit is important, agreeability less so. The best employees can be those who share the same fundamental beliefs and values yet approach issues in unique ways and provide different and fresh perspectives.

CONTRIBUTING AND ENGAGING

ONBOARDING
Everyone Needs a Tour Guide

Create a Formal Process

EMPLOYEE ENGAGEMENT & RETENTION STRATEGIES
Deploy Pulse Surveys

Use Gamification and Scoreboards

Extend Inclusion Externally

Communicate Wins

Onboarding

When I was a freshman at George Washington University, a Latina sorority on campus published a little guidebook that told Latinx students where we could buy homemade tacos and pupusas, which grocery stores carried the foods we were accustomed to buying, where to get our hair done, and when Latin Night was at local venues. Because I was coming to D.C. from New York City, this guidebook helped me feel welcomed in a predominantly White institution. Similarly, new employees to organizations need formal and informal guides so they can feel a connection to their new teams and gain their bearings in an unfamiliar environment.

Most organizations have some manner of onboarding process, but the experience isn't consistent across all new hires. Some teams might adhere to an exact process; other teams might point someone to their desk and consider the job done. The key to onboarding is ensuring it is not just a robust process on paper but that it lives "off the page" in the organization's teams and people.

This same statement can be made about all components of the Talent Lifecycle, but in my experience, the variation exists most robustly in onboarding, which can be a critical inflection point for diverse employees. Both the hiring manager and applicant have worked hard to get to this point in the Talent Lifecycle, so don't let an informal, inconsistent, or nonexistent onboarding process derail progress.

Everyone Needs a Tour Guide

Just as my sorority did with their guidebook, help new employees navigate their new environment, particularly your organization's processes. Pay special attention to opportunities for making initial connections. Institute a process for matching new hires with a "guide," somebody outside their chain of command who can help them learn the ins and outs of your culture. That guide can be a person from the employee-resource groups for diverse hires or someone aligned to one of those groups.

Create a Formal Process

Some organizations rely almost entirely on informal onboarding from colleagues and the team, and anytime something is informal, bias can creep in. Create more formal benchmarking and timelines. Create a simple checklist for both the new hire and their manager. Build in commensurate organizational structures, whether it is an orientation or initial training session or an online database.

ANNE

I've seen organizations focus on attracting and recruiting great talent but miss the mark at retaining that very same talent. Onboarding of talent is much more than just training or ensuring that new hires have the right tools and technology. It's about team and cultural assimilation as well. Too often, the focus is on what the new team member needs to get done, with no help as to how they can go about doing that or who is available to help them.

An approach we have used across our business that I've also seen other companies utilize are new-employee programs. Over the years, we've created programs that span areas such as leadership development, technical development, financial leadership, data analytics, cybersecurity, B2B sales development, and more. These programs typically last anywhere from half a year to several years—and through them, we're able to focus on training, team building, mentoring, and development, as well as provide a broader strategic perspective to our business in the early stage of an employee's experiences. Some programs also include multimonth to annual rotations to expose the employee to diverse experiences and people—again, very early in their careers. It's imperative that these programs provide not only great "during the program" experiences, but also follow-up connection to the "graduated classes" as well—as these cohorts of employees represent key members of your workforce.

Every leader should devote time to employee development, engagement, and retention. These are all inextricably intertwined. Think about it. If I'm not in an environment where I'm growing and learning, or if I'm in an environment where I'm not engaged (i.e., I don't care as much and have less stake in outcomes), or if I have no loyalty to the group, am I really going to be performing at my best? Am I really going to be contributing, innovating, and focusing on moving the business forward? Obviously not.

Here's the key to employee development, engagement, and retention. It's *not* one size fits all. If you hire diverse candidates but fail to foster this diversity and ensure that unconscious biases aren't working against the candidates, be assured, those biases will hold you back. How can you tell? Look at the data. Are you making progress where you need to? where you want to? If not, ask why. And put rigor, commitment, and sponsorship in place to address it.

Employee Engagement and Retention Strategies

During the recession of the early 2000s, many organizations found themselves tightening their belts. They got rid of everything but the necessities as they saw them, including learning and development and initiatives aimed at driving employee engagement. As a result, talent stagnated in many organizations, and as the economy recovered, firms like FranklinCovey saw an outpouring of clients asking for support in building employee-engagement and retention strategies. As the economy recovered and unemployment declined, the bar was raised around employee experience. If we align this to FranklinCovey's Performance Model, we can restate this to say employees could demand a High-Performance Zone where they felt valued, respected, and included.

We have now talked through the High-Performance Zone, and we each know what it feels like to be in that zone and how to create a High-Performance Zone as a leader. Another way to gauge whether an employee is in high performance is through the Levels of Engagement model.

Think about an upcoming project. Where would you rate yourself on this model in regard to that project? Do you feel willing cooperation,

heartfelt commitment, and creative excitement, or do you sense indifferent compliance, resentful obedience, or rebellion and the urge to quit?

The levels of engagement are deliberate—below the dotted line, people are not engaged; they may or may not comply. Above the dotted line there are various levels of engagement, from cheerful cooperation to creative excitement. As we consider employee engagement and retention strategies, it's impossible to be above the line if you are in the Limiting or Damaging Zone. Our goal is to create the conditions where people will be engaged far more often at a level above the line. So, what employee-engagement and retention strategies build that sense of inclusion?

Deploy Pulse Surveys

As Anne mentioned earlier, feedback is a gift. Many organizations have an annual employee-engagement survey or culture assessment. There is usually a corresponding communications campaign pushing people to respond, an unveiling of the results, and a committee given the responsibility to bring about the desired results. While these large-scale efforts can point to organizational trends in problematic behavior or leadership and highlight organizational strengths, they can be cumbersome for smaller organizations to implement and difficult to act on, depending on the scope of the results. In addition, the decision to even conduct such a survey doesn't sit with leaders at all levels, but usually with the executive team or chief human resources officer.

As a leader, consider how you can implement a constant feedback loop through bite-size pulse surveys. At the conclusion of a project, the start of a new quarter, or a month into a new role, send your team a two-to five-question survey. Be clear about your sincere interest in creating a high-performance environment and transparent about the results and what you can implement. For example, at the conclusion of a project, you might send the project team the following:

1. What was your level of engagement in this project?

2. If less than creative excitement, what could I have done to move you up the scale?

3. Did you feel included, valued, and respected? Why or why not?

You might choose to use more pointed questions like:

1. Were you satisfied with the outcome of this project?

2. Did you feel that your voice was heard throughout the project?

3. Was your contribution adequately recognized?

As is true of all the strategies in this book, adjust this idea to suit your leadership style and your organizational culture. Remember that an open door is not a policy, it's just a door. If we want employees to feel engaged, we need to be proactive about asking for their experiences and flexible enough to implement what we hear.

Use Gamification and Scoreboards

When I transitioned almost a decade ago from the public sector to my role at FranklinCovey in the private sector, I was told there would be many differences and braced myself for the change. As a member of the sales team in my role as global client partner, I receive a daily scoreboard tracking my progress in revenue and comparing it to that of my peers. My colleague Chris McChesney, bestselling author of *The 4 Disciplines of Execution,* says, "Nothing drives morale and engagement more than winning." In my public-sector roles, I was often left to gauge my level of success by how my leader felt about me. This is not to say that the public sector can't quantify results. It certainly can and is increasingly asked to do so. This is only to say that when I joined FranklinCovey, it was the first time in my professional career that I felt in control of whether or not I was winning. Winning was very clearly and publicly based on my performance, and the daily scoreboard become like a game to me, a competitive exercise in moving up the board. Earlier in my work life, I felt that a sense of winning or losing mostly came from management and was tied to my being too much of something: too young, too fat, too pregnant, too Black, too opinionated—just too much.

Think about ways you can build a winnable game into your team. In his work on execution, Chris also says employees are engaged by a "winnable game" and are often even more engaged if they played a part in building that game. Does your team know what game they are playing? Are you keeping score in a quantitative way?

Scoreboards remove your preferences and judgments from the equation. For instance, before I had received training in public speaking, if someone asked me how many times I said "um" in a keynote address, I would have said one or two. When someone actually counted, it was more like two *dozen.* If we remove subjectivity by creating a winnable game, our decisions about performance are less about how someone makes us feel and more about the results they achieve. Gamifying the work also ensures that employees know what winning looks like and can work toward that; success is no longer something more subjective, like the communication preferences of a particular leader.

Extend Inclusion Externally

We've talked about the power of seeing yourself reflected in the leadership ranks of an organization. Employees also want to see themselves reflected in the work the organization is doing, be it a multicultural marketing initiative or corporate social-responsibility programs such as sustainability initiatives, employee volunteer programs, and donations to charity. Extending your inclusion goals beyond the organization reinforces your commitment to it. This bolsters the organization's authenticity in the eyes of its employees and supports employee engagement and retention.

Communicate Wins

Leaders tend to vastly undercommunicate their vision. This is true of everything from organizational strategy to commitment to certain initiatives, including diversity and inclusion. I was recently helping a client's chief human resources officer with their strategic rollout of our *Unconscious Bias* work session, and she revealed to me that the organization's employees didn't believe diversity and inclusion were a priority to leadership. Later she mentioned she'd just completed a briefing to the board of directors about the firm's inclusion strategy, and members of the board had been so impressed, they asked if they could share this strategy with other boards on which they served. I asked, "Why is this a secret? Why don't your employees know this is happening?" Your employees can react only to what they see. So, particularly as we consider retention, if employees are leaving because they don't see themselves reflected in the leadership ranks or because their specific manager doesn't support their voice or diversity more broadly, awareness of the larger organizational strategy could have an impact.

Chapter 15: Contributing and Engaging
Reflection for Individuals

1. Reflect on your experiences around Contributing and Engaging. Have you personally experienced (or seen other examples) where an individual's ability to contribute was made through the lens of bias? If so, what was the impact to you and others involved?

   ....

   ....

   ....

   ....

2. How does operating through a lens of performance mitigate possible Contributing and Engaging biases?

   ....

   ....

   ....

   ....

3. How might assignments, work processes, distribution of tools and equipment, or other aspects of the day-to-day workflow when applied through the lens of bias decrease morale, discretionary effort, and retention?

   ....

   ....

   ....

   ....

Chapter 15: Contributing and Engagement
Application for Leaders

Consider your culture and practices when it comes to the ways your team contributes and engages with their day-to-day workflow.

1. List the possible biases that might be in play.

....

....

....

....

2. How could an increase in empathy and curiosity add new insight into the costs of such practices?

....

....

....

....

3. Where might you apply careful or bold courage to make a change?

....

....

....

....

....

....

Chapter 16: Moving Up

It isn't how much you know that matters. What matters is how much access you have to what other people know. It isn't just how intelligent your team members are; it is how much of that intelligence you can draw out and put to use.

—Liz Wiseman, bestselling author of *Multipliers*

Decisions in the **Moving Up** stage of the Talent Lifecycle are concerned with performance management, the full spectrum of development opportunities available at an organization, promotions, sponsorship, and succession planning.

MOVING UP

PERFORMANCE MANAGEMENT

Connect Early and Often

Set Goals Together

Give People Stretch Assignments

SUCCESSION PLANNING

Always Have a Short List

Performance Management

In most organizations, orientation to the role of first-line leader includes all of the law and procedure involved—time and attendance, compensation, employee benefits, what you can and cannot ask about, and the annual performance review. But most leaders also know that performance management is more than an annual performance review. Employees thrive on feedback, and bias or even the perception of bias thrives on silence. Meaning, if there is not ongoing performance management—feedback, coaching, and clear expectations—and then the annual performance review is bad, the employee can assume that negative review is based on bias. On the other hand, based on all we know about the cognitive shortcuts in the brain, if you as a manager are not having ongoing performance conversations, you could easily fall into recency bias, negativity bias, the halo effect, or another cognitive shortcut when the annual performance finally does roll around. The good news, like with every component of the Talent Lifecycle, is that we can implement best practices to avoid this eventuality.

MARK

Almost every organization boasts a commitment to employee engagement and the importance of their people. But in some organizations, this can feel like lip service, especially when their scoreboards and key performance indicators (KPIs) are exclusively focused on sales or deliverable metrics such as revenue achieved or average processing time. Many organizations are moving away from the traditional annual performance review based solely on numbers and KPIs and are looking at a more holistic picture. For example, leaders might be meeting the metrics, but really struggling with retention based on a toxic leadership style that has their people feeling diminished and in the Limiting Zone. Some of this toxicity is often tied to issues of unresolved bias. Organizations are increasingly looking at not just *what* was achieved but also *how* it was achieved.

I work with an international petrochemical manufacturing and supply company that includes elements of trust, psychological safety, and belonging in their annual performance reviews. In addition to KPIs, employees are now rated on their ability to effectively communicate, adapt to change, build accountability in their teams, and create a culture of feedback and development. The overall intent is to ensure the organization is in the High-Performance Zone . . . and it's working!

Connect Early and Often

When we have bias against people—linked to their communication style or their motives or some part of their identities—our instinct is not to bother with them. We might toss them to the side, avoiding them until we have to engage with them for their annual performance review. It's not fair to them. And it sets them up for failure—a failure that becomes the manager's self-fulfilling prophecy.

If we're communicating early and often, we're intentionally building connection and moving past whatever the bias might be to focus on the work. Providing frequent feedback can take many forms—from the formal to the informal. It might be as simple as texting a subordinate after a meeting that they did a nice job describing the problem or proposing solutions. For critical feedback, it might be asking the employee to coffee and brainstorming ways to be more effective or organized in the deployment of a project. Using the Levels of Engagement or Performance Model to frame the conversation can also be helpful. Let your employee know that you want to be sure you're on the same page. Where would they rate their level of engagement on the team or with your new quarterly goals? Do they feel like they're in high performance with the other divisions engaged in this project or with you as a leader? These models give us a foundation for having a more robust conversation. And while each of us has a different measure for what we are comfortable sharing at work, finding opportunities to connect personally can ease the transition into feedback conversations. Knowing that someone is working toward a fitness goal, is very interested in a particular hobby, or spends weekends driving across the state for traveling soccer games is helpful in building trust and connection, as well as ensuring you can see them as a whole person in your assessments and feedback.

Set Goals Together

As a leader, you are measured on the results you achieve. But you do not achieve those results directly; you achieve them through others. This distinction is the transition from an individual contributor to a leader. Because that is what you are measured on, it is easy to fall into the trap of being directive. When we consider the role of bias in moving up and all of the data that points to how difficult moving up can be for people of color, women, introverts, people without advanced degrees, or those transitioning from the military to civilian life, for example, setting goals together can ensure bias doesn't creep in. There are many ways to do this. You could set some parameters for a goal and then ask the employee to weigh in on how they can influence that goal or what they think the best way to accomplish that goal is. I mentioned earlier that I had a particularly influential leader in college who made it a point to work with me to set quarterly goals not just for work, but in my personal life. Now, I was a student and she was an educator, so the context was different from a typical workplace. But it could be incredibly valuable, as it was for me and has been since, to not only set goals specific to an employee's current role, but also help that employee set future goals. That might require some support from you. Perhaps this employee would like to be a leader in the future but doesn't currently have a bachelor's degree, which although not required for a leadership role, has informally been a standard for leaders at the organization. You might in this case set a goal around completing a certification program or college courses, and might connect them to HR for access to a tuition-assistance program. A 360-degree assessment is also a possible foundation for this goal-setting conversation. It's one thing to sit someone down and say, "Here's what I've observed." As I'm sure you've experienced, that can quickly devolve into a mismatched conversation with you in the thinking part of your brain and your employee in the emotional or primitive part of their brain as they brace themselves for feedback. Starting with a 360-degree assessment can give you both a broader picture of how the employee's work and temperament are perceived, and as a leader, you can easily position the employee's success as a partnership between you.

Give People Stretch Assignments

One of the informal ways leaders manage performance is through the "inner cadre": they give certain team members stretch assignments or high-visibility opportunities that other people just don't get. To be more intentional about informal performance management, spread the opportunities equally. Ensure that you are not relegating low-profile or administrative tasks to the same group of people; rotate those tasks equally. And as you plan for higher-profile tasks, think beyond delegating to just the go-to members of your team and consider who might be interested in a new challenge. If you have five assignments and five people, deliberately give an assignment to each person.

ANNE

Truth be told, I do not like the notion of "moving up" in one's career. Why? Because I feel that it's tied to the antiquated notion of the "corporate ladder"—a term that implies there's only one motion we should all aspire to, and that's moving up that ladder. In my experience, there is nothing further from the truth. Think about it: If everyone wanted to "move up," most people would "fall off" because there just isn't room at the top of that ladder for everyone.

Rather, I've always viewed that careers are more like a snowflake—where there is no beginning and no end—and importantly, every single one is different. I feel strongly that one's focus should be on moving forward. So what does moving forward mean in one's career and how does bias play a role? I'll share an example from my own career.

I started at AT&T in an engineering role and progressed into operational and product roles. By the time I'd had about four assignments under my belt, several of my mentors told me that I would need to go into sales if I ever aspired to become an executive someday. Honestly, I didn't know what I wanted at that point, but I did know that I didn't want to be limited—so I started pursuing a sales role. (By the way, at the time, most of the top executives in the company had meaningful sales experiences, so that was proof enough for me that the experience might be worthwhile, even though it was something I never aspired to.) I was rejected over and over again. The primary reason given was that there was no way I could be successful because I hadn't started my career in sales. There was also no contingent of engineers turned salespeople in their ranks. Eventually, albeit over the course of three to four years, I managed to get in, and ironically, I've spent half my career now in enterprise sales and service!

Unconscious bias is a powerful thing. People look for role models, and it's natural that they tend to seek role models who appear to be most obviously "like them." This could mean gender identity, ethnicity, education, background, geographic roots, or otherwise. We need to resist our natural inclination to support others who are most like us. Of course, this doesn't mean we shouldn't bring such people forward, but we should purposefully ensure we are diverse in our own thoughts, approach, and actions.

As leaders, we have an obligation to help each of our team members develop a career as robust and rewarding as they desire it to be— remember, no two snowflakes are the same. There is not a "one size fits all" approach to coaching, mentoring, or sponsorship. Each person deserves an opportunity to have a fulfilling career and not be encumbered by unconscious bias. Remember, it's about moving forward—making progress, and feeling and knowing that you are growing. For some, growth and aspiration are manifested in a desire to become a supervisor of a group or the direct leader of a team, organization, or unit. For others, growth and aspiration could be represented in a portfolio of work experiences involving the latest and greatest technologies . . . or in the opportunity to travel and live all around the world . . . or in having a steady role providing the time and energy necessary to pursue parallel contributions in the community or otherwise. You get the gist. Moving forward in one's career should be the goal. Leadership takes on countless forms. And the beauty is that the journey in the pursuit and achievement of fulfillment in one's life is never-ending.

While much progress has been made, there is more work to be done. Every single leader can play an important role in ensuring that biases are brought to light and addressed such that every single member of their team has an opportunity to shine—not just yesterday or today, but into the future. The time is now for each of us to do our part.

Succession Planning

A lot of organizations have diversity only in the lower ranks. The military, for example, is incredibly diverse. It is most diverse in the enlisted ranks and less diverse as you move up through the ranks. There are still places in the military where a woman or a person of color has not yet served in a high-ranking role.

Many organizations struggle with diversity at leadership levels because they don't have anyone to pull from at lower levels. Remember that diversifying your front line is an investment in your future leadership pipeline.

Always Have a Short List

People are caught up in what they need to do, and they're not necessarily considering succession planning. This is actually a best practice we have on our executive team. FranklinCovey requires that each executive must identify two people.

Then push beyond your short list. Go beyond the usual suspects. Refer to the network activity. Ask yourself if the people you want to promote are mirror images of you in any way. Did they come up the same way you did? Did they go to the same schools? Are they the same identity? Consider candidates who may be outside the boundaries of these identifiers.

MARK

Thinking about boundaries, I was recently discussing promotions with a large U.S. healthcare provider. They were recruiting for an "organizational development consultant" and "director of human resources." These hires needed to be driven leaders, operating at a high level. At one point, the conversation turned to the fact that nobody present during the discussion could be promoted above their current level, despite their decades of experience. All positions above a director level required a graduate degree, which nobody in the room had.

In this organization, one of the boundaries for promotion was a graduate degree, and this meant that many of their leadership roles were filled with external candidates. In an organization like this one, we should consider how we build a path to promotion for those who've earned that opportunity through their tenure. In other organizations, the opposite bias might hold true. For example, I work with a large consulting firm that feels very strongly that leaders must be promoted from within because an external candidate could not possibly navigate the internal nuances and structures. Their bias is to value institutional knowledge. They might consider looking at their slate of candidates for promotion and requiring that it include internal and external possibilities.

What potential talent is being overlooked because of biases, both conscious and unconscious, that drive promotion decisions? Are there similar rules in your organization that might be inadvertently narrowing your talent pool and opportunities for your employees?

Where Do You Start?

Let's return to the question I am so often asked: "Where do we start?" When it comes to the Talent Lifecycle, there is no one consistent circumstance. Organizations differ in size, function, demographics, and culture.

The first step is knowing the state of your organization. Map out the Talent Lifecycle at a high level—Getting Hired, Contributing and Engaging, and Moving Up. Then drill down further. What does Getting Hired look like at your organization? What are the formal processes, and what is the informal experience? Challenge yourself not to do any guessing as you work through this. If you don't know, find out. You then have a snapshot of your organization's reality that includes strengths, opportunities, and data yet to gather.

Contributing and Engaging requires collaboration. Too often, the Talent Lifecycle is relegated to HR, but in an ideal circumstance, shifting to high performance in this model requires cross-functional perspectives that include HR, legal, and diversity, equity, and inclusion, as well as leadership at all levels of the organization. Many organizations form a diversity advisory council or other form of senior council to ensure a cross-functional approach. Tackling the Talent Lifecycle is not a job for one person or division. Because it touches every person in the organization, it requires a diversity of perspectives.

Chapter 16: Moving Up
Reflection for Individuals

1. Reflect on your experiences around performance management and promotions. Have you personally experienced (or seen) a situation in which an individual's advancement was made through the lens of bias? If so, what was the impact to you and others involved?

....

....

....

....

2. How does operating through a lens of performance mitigate possible Moving Up biases?

....

....

....

....

3. How might promotion and advancements when made through the lens of bias decrease morale, discretionary effort, and retention?

....

....

....

....

Chapter 16: Moving Up
Application for Leaders

Consider your culture and practices when it comes to how your team members advance and are promoted in your organization.

1. List the possible biases that might be in play.

....

....

....

....

2. How could an increase in empathy and curiosity add new insight concerning the costs of such practices?

....

....

....

....

3. Where might you apply careful or bold courage to make a change?

....

....

....

....

....

Conclusion

If there is no struggle, there is no progress.

—Frederick Douglass, abolitionist and writer

One day my husband, son, and I were driving home from a Saturday afternoon trip to McDonald's in Alexandria, Virginia. My husband and I both held national-security clearances as a result of our work with the U.S. government, and intentionally lived just a few miles from the Pentagon. We noticed a police car behind us, and as we drove the final mile home, it got closer and closer without turning on the sirens. We pulled into our community and into a parking spot in front of our apartment. As my husband put the car in park and we undid our seat belts, the police car dramatically swerved in behind us, angling in a way that wouldn't allow my husband to back up. The officer hopped out of his car, his hand on the holster, reaching for his gun as my five-year-old hopped out of the back seat, near where the officer was standing. I got out of the passenger seat just in time to see my five-year-old standing in front of a police officer with his hand on his gun. I jumped in front of him and asked if there was a problem. Startled, he apologized and said my husband matched the description of a suspect in a crime, who had been seen in a car similar to ours. He asked us a few questions and went on his way. Honest mistake, perhaps, but also frightening against the backdrop of Black boys and men in America. In this instance, I was afraid not for myself, but for my husband and son.

It is undeniable that bias against Black people is quite pervasive in America and an issue every community and law enforcement organization is wrestling with. When we're on the receiving end of bias—be it from individual circumstances or society at large—we can experience the Damaging Zone in dramatically different ways, personally and professionally. The power and importance of taking action to root out bias, conscious and unconscious, cannot be overstated.

MARK

In my role as a senior consultant at FranklinCovey, I'm sometimes at a new client site each day. Over the course of a month, I might be delivering a variety of FranklinCovey solutions at fifteen different firms. Each morning when I walk into the client site, I don't necessarily know the client (if it's my first time working with them), their culture, or their biases. And depending on where it is in the country or the type of firm, I might walk in with my own biases around how they accept or don't accept members of the LGBTQ+ community or Baby Boomers or Texans, for that matter.

This means that almost every day, I have to accelerate the process of moving past bias, because I'm always entering a new environment and meeting new people. My work is guided by first impressions, which, as we've discussed, can be riddled with inaccuracy. As we've mentioned throughout this text, bias can be about a great many things, and in my life, one of the most profound biases I've experienced is around my orientation. I sometimes fall back into that sense of insecurity I had in my youth and hesitate to share this detail of my identity and my life. But I've found that the more appropriately vulnerable I am, the more the ideas I'm responsible for facilitating resonate and the more people are able to be vulnerable about their own biases and experiences with bias. This is how we make progress and grow together.

When I facilitate our *Unconscious Bias* solution, my opening slide is a picture of my boys. Michael is ten and Máximo is four. They are sitting in a large, circular netted swing, the kind you often find in new playgrounds, wearing superhero T-shirts and smiling brightly at me as I capture the rare harmonious moment between brothers. These two motivate me in a way nothing ever has. As counterintuitive as it may seem, some of my biggest professional achievements are tied to these two tiny humans. They make me better!

My responsibility to my boys is to contribute to building a world where they can live without fear of bias, conscious or unconscious—where their possibilities are not limited by any component of their identities. I throw myself at this every day. But the data says that no matter what I do—the neighborhood we live in, the house we own, the schools I send them to, the volume of books on our shelves, the two-parent home and education and income my husband and I make—their outcomes may still be less than those of their White peers. That is the reality of being the mother of two Black boys in America. This reality, my reality, is why conversations about inclusion and bias are so important to me.

ANNE

The work of reframing bias, cultivating connection, and creating high-performance teams is about elevating the whole—the whole person, the whole team, the whole organization, the whole community, and ultimately the whole world.

I didn't understand what this really meant until well into my career. In fact, as I reflect on my childhood and early adulthood, I spent an immense amount of time and energy trying to be who others thought I was or should be. As a child, I straddled two worlds, wanting to make my parents proud, while also wanting so badly to fit in and "be popular." At home, I experienced cultural, generational, and language gaps with my parents, and at school, I felt like an anomaly.

Fast-forward into my early career, and while I was doing well by all measures, I wasn't fully authentic or able to show up as a whole person. I felt pressure at work to behave in a certain way to fit in. Based on my upbringing, I felt the need to suppress my voice, even when I knew I had more to contribute. I was in the Limiting Zone. But I'd seen my parents' journey as first-generation Americans and the perseverance, resilience, and courage they'd demonstrated, constantly getting back up after being knocked down. I couldn't be my whole self without embracing that same grit. And ultimately, I learned that in order to really connect with others, I had to get over this desire to "fit." I needed to connect authentically with my whole self first. That meant embracing my flaws and weaknesses as well as my strengths and passions. And yes, it also meant a constant exploration of my biases.

I challenge and encourage you to do the same: embrace your whole self and confront and bring to light your unconscious biases. We all have them. It's totally normal. But until we make them visible and begin to understand them, we won't be able to constructively work through them. And we won't be able to fully realize our greatest potential or help others do so as well so that, collectively, we can make the most significant positive impact possible.

As a leader, you can have a profound impact at work, across your community, and in the world. As individuals, we each have unique experiences, skills, and perspectives through which we can apply the practices outlined in this book. Our strength lies in both our similarities and our differences, and progress can always be made—together. In fact, I fundamentally believe that in order to drive, motivate, and inspire systemic sustainable change, we must do so together. That is the beauty and power of humanity. We are, indeed, better together.

Bias, equity, diversity, and inclusion have always been important issues to the effectiveness and engagement of a workforce. The Civil Rights Act prohibiting discrimination based on race, color, religion, sex, and national origin was passed in 1964. If you were born the year this legislation passed, you would be fifty-six in 2020. That's not that long ago. Before 1978 and the passage of the Pregnancy Discrimination Act, women could be fired for being pregnant without protection under the law. It took another twelve years for workplace protections to extend to people with disabilities with the Americans with Disabilities Act of 1990. While there was some effort to reintegrate Vietnam veterans into the workforce in the late sixties and seventies, it wasn't until the 2000s that we saw widespread hiring initiatives for veterans across the public and private sector in an attempt to reintegrate veterans of the Iraq and Afghanistan wars. In the United States, victims of workplace discrimination and harassment based on sexual orientation/gender identity were not protected federally until June 2020.

With each of these policy shifts, we saw the workforce expand. And with each change in the composition or demographics of the workforce, we also see a need to address bias—the biases that the legacy workforce and the new workforce have about one another. These biases can take over the organizational culture, and this is not an issue trending downward. This will be an ongoing challenge as the demographics of our society shift and change over time. As Baby Boomers continue to work, there is incredible bias around their ongoing contribution. As Gen Z enters the workforce, there is bias around how they communicate and expectations. The 2018 U.S. Census Bureau data showed that for the first time, non-Hispanic White residents made up less than half of the nation's population under age fifteen, and demographers project that White people will become a minority in the United States by 2045.* The way in which our society and the workplace view the contribution of people with disabilities of all kinds and neurodiversity in particular means we need to reimagine work to accommodate the priorities of this talented group. Many organizations are focused on how to stay relevant and tap into the best talent in light of future demographics. This includes second careers and working proactively to address the concerns of a more experienced professional transitioning to a new industry, a parent or eldercare provider reentering the workforce after a time away, and of course veterans.

These details are not meant to overwhelm you but instead to highlight how timeless and really evergreen the issue of bias is. The specifics will evolve, but bias will remain a natural part of the human condition and of our relationships to one another. Reframing how we think about bias, cultivating meaningful connection, and choosing courage will ensure we are always poised to build high-performing teams.

Leadership is a high calling, and in its toughest moments, when we're in the management trenches, we must remind ourselves that this is both a privilege and important work. The late Harvard Business School professor Clayton Christensen wrote that "done well, management is

---

* William H. Frey, "Less Than Half of US Children Under 15 Are White, Census Shows." Brookings, June 24, 2019; www.brookings.edu/research/less-than-half -of-us-children-under-15-are-white-census-shows/.

among the most noble of professions," because of the significant day-to-day influence we have on the well-being of our employees, their families, and our communities.

Many of us fancy ourselves *great* leaders. We understand the importance of leading from where we are, using both formal and informal authority and building trust with our people. Fewer of us define ourselves as *inclusive* leaders. But leadership cannot be effective without inclusion. This has always been the case and will continue to be.

As authors, we're often asked how we'll know we've been successful in equity, diversity, and inclusion in the workplace. We believe we'll have been successful when every leader in every organization ties their feelings about these ideas to performance. We need to constantly be making that shift to the High-Performance Zone, ensuring that everyone across the organization, from top to bottom, feels valued, included, and respected. If that's not the case, there's still work to do and we're missing out on the full contribution those individuals can make to our organizations.

Of course we all have a lot to do, and we're responsible for more than we can sometimes bear. As leaders, we're trying to conduct efficient meetings, present persuasively, increase revenues, satisfy customers, innovate, reorganize the company and, ultimately, deliver results. The only way leaders will apply the behaviors we've talked about in this book, work through the tools, and add this lens of bias to their actions, interactions, and decisions is if they truly believe in the value that diversity, inclusion, and the conquest of our limiting biases bring to our organizational culture.

To make progress on bias in the midst of your already busy leadership career, you must have a reason to make room for this as a priority in your life. Your reason doesn't need to look like my reason (my boys), or Mark's reason (a sense of worthiness and value), or Anne's (the experience of straddling two worlds). In fact, it's unlikely that it will.

In this book, you have hopefully uncovered some sparks of insight or resonance. Think more about those. Build out the story of why this subject matters to you. And with that point of connection, take action and implement positive change.

Conclusion
Reflection for Individuals

Addressing unconscious bias is tough work—don't forget to stop and acknowledge your progress. Celebrate the wins, both incremental and breakthrough. Have you built a five-minute meditation practice? Have you sought out feedback on bias and handled it gracefully? Have you volunteered in your community? Jot down your wins each week, and share your progress with a mentor or friend.

Revisit your responses to the tools at the end of each chapter and the commitments you made. Then keep going.

1. What small practice will you institute to make progress on bias?

....

....

2. How will you celebrate when you've made it a habit?

....

....

3. Identify an opportunity for your team or organization to make progress on unconscious bias—such as creating a mentorship program, instituting a devil's advocate role in decision-making meetings, or using gender-neutral language in your employee handbook. Discuss your idea with your leader during your next 1-on-1. Don't forget to plan how you'll celebrate when you see this idea come to life.

....

....

....

Conclusion
Application for Leaders

If you've been working on the issue of unconscious bias with your team, it's even more important to celebrate progress. Set a big goal like creating a hiring panel to replace 1-on-1 interviews or instituting an "Email-Free Tuesday" to build connection—then determine how you'll celebrate once you achieve it. For smaller wins, carve out a regular time in a weekly meeting for the team to share progress.

1. What small change could your team institute to make progress on unconscious bias?

....

....

....

2. What big goal could your team set to make progress on unconscious bias?

....

....

....

3. How will you celebrate when you've achieved it?

....

....

....

....

....

Acknowledgments

Pamela Fuller

This is for my Papi, who taught me to demand my place in the world; for the teacher who told me I'd publish a book one day; for Cicely Washington, who knew I wrote all of our group projects; for the many colleagues at FranklinCovey who believe in the importance of this work and my ability to give it voice—Julienne Stathis, Preston Luke, Chris Miller, Brittany Forbes, Vivien Price, Catherine Nelson, Scott Miller, and Meg Hackett (to name a few)—and for my incredible husband and inspiring boys who prop me up each day: Thank you!

Mark Murphy

For my family of origin: my parents and my siblings, Scott, Leslie, and Tiffany, without whose unwavering support I wouldn't be here to share my thoughts. For my family of choice: especially Tim, Keith, Jorge, and Eileen, who've been by my side for most of the adventures in my life and are constantly showing me what true friendship means. For my FranklinCovey professional family: the leaders, client partners, consultants, and clients who for the past twenty-nine years have taught me the importance of bringing my authentic self to the workplace!

Anne Chow

To the numerous colleagues I've worked with throughout my career, I'm thankful for our relationships and shared experiences. This project is about paying it forward. To the team at FranklinCovey, I'm deeply appreciative for inclusion in this vital work enabling teams to move forward more powerfully together. Finally, to my family, my deepest gratitude. For my parents, Ming and Joann, your countless sacrifices. My husband, Bob, for everything. And for my daughters, Alana and Camryn, for the gift of you. Make the future bright, for others and for yourselves.

Index

Page numbers in *italics* refer to illustrations; those followed by "n" indicate footnotes.

About FranklinCovey

FranklinCovey is a global public company specializing in organizational-performance improvement. We help organizations and individuals achieve results that require a change in human behavior. Our expertise is in seven areas: leadership, execution, productivity, trust, sales performance, customer loyalty, and education. FranklinCovey clients have included 90 percent of the Fortune 100, more than 75 percent of the Fortune 500, thousands of small and midsize businesses, as well as numerous government entities and educational institutions. FranklinCovey has more than 100 direct and partner offices providing professional services in more than 160 countries and territories.

About the Authors

Pamela Fuller is FranklinCovey's thought leader on unconscious bias, lead architect of its organizational solution, and one of the firm's top global sales leaders. Pamela served as an architect of FranklinCovey's *Unconcious Bias* work session and has delivered that session, as well as DEI strategy discussions, to thousands of leaders around the globe. She is also responsible for helping clients customize and implement learning and organizational-development solutions to meet their strategic objectives across FranklinCovey's full catalog of learning solutions.

After earning her MBA, Pamela served as a diversity analyst at the U.S. Department of Defense, focusing on human capital planning, diversity training, and statistical workforce analysis. She began her career in nonprofit fundraising and advocacy, always connected to inclusion and the voice of marginalized groups. Pamela currently lives in South Florida with her husband and children, where they spend their free time exploring all manner of superheroes.

Mark Murphy is a FranklinCovey senior consultant who has facilitated content successfully to clients worldwide for almost three decades.

Through his own life experiences and extensive global travel, Mark is passionate about inclusion and bias, and is an expert in helping clients create diversity in their cultures. He has helped organizations build effective and inclusive cultures in the public sector, Fortune 500 companies, and the U.S. government.

Mark is an expert in helping clients drive culture change. He works with clients to develop and execute strategies aligned to the client's mission and vision that help drive large-scale behavior change all the way to the front line. Mark is phenomenal at developing leaders and individual contributors so organizations can meet their goals and reach new levels of effectiveness.

Mark grew up in Colorado and has called Dallas home since 1994.

Anne Chow is the chief executive officer of AT&T Business. She leads an organization of more than 30,000 employees responsible for serving nearly 3 million business customers around the globe representing over $35 billion in revenues. With decades in the industry, Anne has led numerous global organizations through major transformations and developed countless role-model relationships with clients, partners, and colleagues along the way. She's known for being a professional and personal trailblazer and champion and catalyst for change in numerous circles. In addition to building world-class teams with winning cultures, Anne is also passionate about education, diversity and inclusion, advancing women in technology, and cultivating next-generation leaders. With a master's in business administration with distinction from the Johnson Graduate School of Management at Cornell University and a BS and a master's in electrical engineering from Cornell, Anne is also a graduate of the Pre-College Division of the Juilliard School of Music. A transplanted Jersey girl, Anne currently lives in the Dallas area with her husband and daughters.

Bring This Content Into Your Organization

To learn more about how FranklinCovey's *Unconscious Bias* work session can support your team and organization, visit franklincovey.com/Solutions/unconscious-bias

Bias is a natural part of the human condition—of how the brain works. But it affects how we make decisions, engage with others, and respond to various situations and circumstances, often limiting potential. *Unconscious Bias: Understanding Bias to Unleash Potential*™ helps participants:

- **Identify Bias** where it shows up in our own thinking and in our workplaces.
- **Cultivate Connection** with those around us to expand our understanding and improve our decision making.
- **Choose Courage** as we engage with care and boldness in addressing biases that limit people and constrain performance.

There is nothing more fundamental to performance than how we see and treat each other as human beings. Helping your leaders and team members address bias will let them thrive, increasing performance across your organization.

Content can be delivered Live In-Person, Live-Online, and On Demand.

FRANKLINCOVEY
ON LEADERSHIP
WITH
SCOTT MILLER

Join executive vice president Scott Miller for weekly interviews with thought leaders, bestselling authors, and world-renowned experts on the topics of organizational culture, leadership development, execution, and personal productivity.

FEATURED INTERVIEWS INCLUDE:

GUY KAWASAKI
WISE GUY

KIM SCOTT
RADICAL CANDOR

SETH GODIN
THE DIP, LINCHPIN, PURPLE COW

LIZ WISEMAN
MULTIPLIERS

STEPHEN M. R. COVEY
THE SPEED OF TRUST

STEDMAN GRAHAM
IDENTITY LEADERSHIP

GENERAL STANLEY McCHRYSTAL
LEADERS: MYTH AND REALITY

SUSAN DAVID
EMOTIONAL AGILITY

DANIEL PINK
WHEN

NELY GALÁN
SELF MADE

RACHEL HOLLIS
GIRL, WASH YOUR FACE

NANCY DUARTE
DATA STORY, SLIDE:OLOGY

STEPHANIE McMAHON
CHIEF BRAND OFFICER, WWE

ANNE CHOW
CEO, AT&T BUSINES

Subscribe to FranklinCovey's *On Leadership* to receive weekly videos, tools, articles, and podcasts at

FRANKLINCOVEY.COM/ONLEADERSHIP.

SCHEDULE A SPEAKER
FOR YOUR NEXT EVENT

PAMELA FULLER   MARK MURPHY   ANNE CHOW

Are you planning an event for your organization? Schedule one of the authors of *The Leader's Guide to Unconscious Bias* to deliver an engaging keynote or work session tailored to your leaders or audience.

- Association and Industry Conferences
- Sales Conferences
- Annual Meetings
- Leadership Development

- Executive and Board Retreats
- Company Functions
- Onsite Consulting
- Client Engagements

These experts have spoken at hundreds of conferences and client events worldwide.

To schedule a speaker today, call
1-888-554-1776
or visit franklincovey.com/speakers-bureau.